ESSENTIALS *of* LAW *and* ETHICS *for* PHARMACY TECHNICIANS

SECOND EDITION

CRC PRESS
PHARMACY
EDUCATION
SERIES

ESSENTIALS *of* LAW *and* ETHICS *for* PHARMACY TECHNICIANS

SECOND EDITION

KENNETH M. STRANDBERG

CRC Press
Taylor & Francis Group
Boca Raton   London   New York

CRC Press is an imprint of the
Taylor & Francis Group, an informa business

CRC Press
Taylor & Francis Group
6000 Broken Sound Parkway NW, Suite 300
Boca Raton, FL 33487-2742

© 2007 by Taylor & Francis Group, LLC
CRC Press is an imprint of Taylor & Francis Group, an Informa business

No claim to original U.S. Government works
Printed in the United States of America on acid-free paper
10 9 8 7 6 5 4 3 2 1

International Standard Book Number-10: 1-4200-4556-3 (Softcover)
International Standard Book Number-13: 978-1-4200-4556-7 (Softcover)

Library of Congress Cataloging-in-Publication Data

Strandberg, Kenneth M.
  Essentials of law and ethics for pharmacy technicians / author, Kenneth M. Strandberg. -- 2nd ed.
      p. ; cm. -- (CRC Press pharmacy education series.)
  "A CRC title."
  Includes bibliographical references and index.
  ISBN-13: 978-1-4200-4556-7 (hardcover : alk. paper)
  ISBN-10: 1-4200-4556-3 (hardcover : alk. paper)
      1. Pharmacy--Law and legislation--United States. 2. Pharmacists--Legal status, laws, etc.--United States. 3. Pharmacy technicians--Professional ethics--United States. I. Title.

  KF2915.P452S77 2007
  344.7304'16--dc22   2006102484

Visit the Taylor & Francis Web site at
http://www.taylorandfrancis.com

and the CRC Press Web site at
http://www.crcpress.com

PREFACE

Although many excellent textbooks deal with pharmacy laws, regulations, and ethics, all of those currently marketed are aimed at the university-level pharmacy student. During my years as a faculty member and as a department chair, the lack of textbooks intended for pharmacy technicians became more and more noticeable, especially after visiting with pharmacy technician faculty and our colleagues at Pharmacy Technician Educator's Council (PTEC) meetings. The standard practice seems to be to incorporate law and ethics material into other classes, using parts of these university-level textbooks and articles and adding extra lecture time and materials. Few programs have a stand-alone law and ethics course or even a segment of such a course, which can perhaps be explained by the fact that no text has been aimed at this need. Instructors have been forced to "make do" with material and resources that are meant for an entirely different group of students.

This book attempts to fill this gap by covering topics of which pharmacy technicians should be aware to practice in a manner that is both legal and ethical. A large part of a technician's duty is to be aware of the law's requirements and restrictions. This awareness takes much of that worry away from the pharmacist; exposure to education in ethics frees a person's mind to act in a manner that is loyal to one's own standards and to the expectations and obligations of serving people's health needs. This book brings these together in one resource in a manner that is appropriate to a technician's practice and role.

ACKNOWLEDGMENTS

A special thank you must go to those who have granted me the privilege of reprinting their copyrighted material. The Philadelphia College of Pharmacy, the American Pharmaceutical Association, the American Association of Colleges of Pharmacy, the American Association of Pharmacy Technicians, the American Hospital Association, the American Society of Health-System Pharmacists, and the National Association of Boards of Pharmacy were all most cooperative and helpful in making available their reserved material for reproduction and use here.

I am grateful for the support of several people in this project: Barbara Lacher, RPhTech, CPhT, assistant program director of the Pharmacy Technician Program at the North Dakota State College of Science, for her guidance and ideas; my students at North Dakota State University's College of Pharmacy and at the North Dakota State College of Science Pharmacy Technician Program for their questions and input; and my dean at NDSU, Dr. Charles Peterson, my dean at NDSCS, Mr. Ken Kompelein, and my former dean at NDSCS, Mr. Harvey Link, for their consistent faith in me.

A special thank you is reserved for my brother, Dr. Lee R. Strandberg, professor emeritus of the Oregon State University College of Pharmacy and currently director of managed care pharmacy for the Samaritan Health System of Corvallis, Oregon. While I was an undergraduate searching for a major, his suggestion led me to pharmacy school and, since I started teaching at NDSU part time in 1988, he has readily come to my aid with advice, guidance, and material. He has played a significant positive role in my professional life.

AUTHOR

Kenneth M. Strandberg is the program director of the Pharmacy Technician Program at the North Dakota State College of Science in Wahpeton, North Dakota, a position he has held since 1994. This program has certificate and associate degree options, both available via on-campus and distance-learning options (both paper based and Web based). Since 1988, he has also been an adjunct professor of pharmacy practice at North Dakota State University in Fargo and an adjunct assistant professor of medicine at the University of North Dakota School of Medicine in Grand Forks. He has retired as the pharmacy department manager at a Veterans Administration hospital and clinic and is now the associate director for scientific affairs at PRACS Institute, a pharmaceutical research firm. He received his bachelor of science in pharmacy in 1974 and master's of business administration in 1984, both from North Dakota State University.

Professor Strandberg's main lecture interests are pharmacy law, pharmacy innovation, and entrepreneurship. He conducts classes in law at NDSCS and in innovation and entrepreneurship as well as pharmacy management at NDSU. He has published several articles and given seminars on pharmacy law and regulations.

He is a member of the Pharmacy Technician Educator's Council, the American Society of Health-System Pharmacists, the North Dakota Pharmaceutical Association, the North Dakota Society of Health-System Pharmacists, and several other local professional associations.

CONTENTS

1

THE LEGAL SYSTEM IN THE UNITED STATES

OVERVIEW AND OBJECTIVES

The practice of pharmacy is one of the most regulated activities in our society. Imagine, just based on the difference in laws and regulations applying to the two endeavors, how much simpler it is to operate a card-and-gift shop than to operate a pharmacy. Pharmacy laws and regulations are so extensive because of the basic nature of our work. We routinely handle substances for which an error in dispensing can be fatal, and an error in distribution, shipping, or purchasing could result in the availability of dangerous drugs on the street through illegal, unregulated channels. To practice within legal limits, pharmacists have much to remember. Most of these limits and requirements have resulted from problems that occurred in the past or have been put into place in an effort to avoid improper events.

Legal issues are often difficult to see as either right or wrong because most things are not simply black or white; there is a broad gray zone in the legal system's interpretation of laws and regulations. If laws and regulations were always simply yes or no, black or white, true or false, courts, judges, and lawyers would not be needed very often. However, circumstances that could affect the legality or motivation of an action and therefore change the way something is viewed by the legal system usually surround an event. Most often, common sense wins out, and the right thing to do is obvious, but sometimes extra steps should be taken to do what is best for the patient and still do what society expects of us. Society's opinions are spelled out in a nation's laws and regulations, and when there is a disagreement, these opinions are interpreted by the courts. Pharmacy personnel have a dual challenge in daily practice in that they must abide by society's opinion of what is proper conduct by obeying the laws and regulations and they also must do what is ethically right for the patient's proper care.

Chapter 1 discusses the following subjects:

- Legislation and legislative bodies
- Regulations and administrative regulatory agencies
- Court actions and interpretations
- Criminal prosecutions and civil lawsuits
- Malpractice

LEGISLATION, REGULATION, AND INTERPRETATION

Laws as they exist in their final form have been enacted as a result of three factors:

1. The actions of a legislative group
2. The actions of a government administrative agency
3. The actions of the courts

Each of these, in its own way, creates requirements of our behavior, and taken together, the actions of all these bodies govern one's performance. Legislative groups, such as state legislatures or the federal Congress, are made up of people elected to make decisions on our behalf; the laws they pass are called *statutes*. Statutes are mostly laws that direct administrative agencies, such as the state board of pharmacy or the federal Food and Drug Administration, to determine how to accomplish something and then do it. As such, they are often called *enabling legislation* because the law enables an agency to do something that needs to be done.

Clearly, neither the state legislature nor federal Congress has the time or knowledge to control and monitor every little detail of every law, such as where to place stop signs, what kind of eye test should be used for a driver's license exam, who should be allowed to dispense medications, or how we should keep records of continuing education classes. They leave it up to the administrative agency to take care of those details, which gives the administrative agency its power to create regulations that the citizens must obey. At this stage, it is easiest for people to influence these events for, during the process of making regulations, the administrative agencies ask interested people to comment on the proposed regulations. The agency must consider all comments while forming the final draft of the regulation, and comments from individual citizens are routinely incorporated into regulations.

Three considerations determine whether a regulation is legal:

1. Does the agency have the authority to regulate a given topic? Obviously, a state board of pharmacy has authority to regulate pharmacy-related legislation, but does it have the authority to regulate some of the actions of a physician? Of a nurse? Of a police officer? Of a convenience store clerk? Of a TV repairman? Of a barber? Some of these people, depending on the specific situation, could be affected by pharmacy regulations, but others are clearly beyond the scope of authority of a board of pharmacy.
2. Is there a statute that gives the agency the authority to regulate a specific subject? Before an agency's actions can be considered legal, there must be a statute to direct it to carry out such actions. This direction can be quite broad, perhaps just stating that pharmacists and technicians must complete an "adequate amount of continuing education activities" to keep their license. It is then up to the state board to determine what that means and how to accomplish it, which usually results in several pages of requirements and directions.
3. Does the regulation address the public health, safety, and welfare? Regulations must be pertinent to be appropriate. Requiring all pharmacy personnel to wear a certain type of clothing is not an appropriate thing to regulate but requiring them to clean their work surfaces with isopropyl alcohol or another approved disinfectant is.

Regulatory agencies provide the detail work of governing, and it is here that citizens have the greatest influence — from serving on the advisory boards or the regulatory board itself to giving input on topics under consideration. Federal agencies inform the public of an opportunity to comment by publishing their proposed regulations in the *Federal Register*, a daily publication that includes all proposed regulations, final regulations and notices. The proposed regulation is printed, and an address to which citizens can send comments is provided, allowing anyone an opportunity to express an opinion on the proposal. Once a regulation is made final, it is published in a subsequent issue of the *Federal Register* and in the *Code of Federal Regulations*, an annual publication of all finalized regulations divided into subject areas referred to as *titles*. For example, all regulations of the Food and Drug Administration are in Title 21.

The third factor that affects the law and how it regulates behavior is court decisions. Courts enter into the picture when one of two things occurs:

1. There is a dispute between two or more people or parties. This is where the ancient principle of common law applies. *Common law* is the history of resolved disputes in a court's area of authority (referred to as its *jurisdiction*). It gives our legal system a set of precedents that allow for continuity or predictability in court decisions based on what was decided in similar situations in the past.

2. There is a question of the interpretation of the law or regulation, that is, what was really intended when this statute or regulation was written. Here, courts will attempt to determine what the intent of the legislature, Congress, or state board was at the time the statute or regulation was passed and whether it applies to the problem at hand. The court may go so far as to read the minutes of meetings to determine the intent. At other times, the court will conclude that the current situation had no precedent, and the court will have to decide, based on its own interpretation of legislative intent, how to apply the law to today's world.

Courts have the final say on what the law really means, and law schools recognize this by requiring that students intensively study past court cases. By referring to past decisions, lawyers determine how they are going to handle a problem and to influence the way a current situation is managed.

CRIMINAL VERSUS CIVIL LAW

Courts can address a problem as either a criminal problem or a civil issue, and because of the fundamental differences between the two concepts, someone who violates the law can be prosecuted in both ways at the same time.

Criminal law deals with the relationship between the individual and society as a whole. It is called into action when people break a law. They have done something against all of society, and they are prosecuted by the government's attorneys for breaking the law. For example, if people steal, then the state can prosecute them for the theft as a criminal act.

Civil law is called on when the relationship between individuals presents problems. Its two segments are contracts and torts. *Contracts* are agreements into which two or more people enter. For example, a painter may agree to paint a house for a certain amount of money, and if it is not done or not done right, then the homeowner could sue the painter for not living up to the agreement. This type of suit is called a *breach of contract*. *Torts* are obligations that the law enforces between two or more people. For example, pharmacists must dispense the right medication as prescribed. Civil lawsuits are prosecuted by attorneys hired by people who feel they were treated wrongly. Government lawyers are not involved.

A person can be prosecuted by both a criminal proceeding and a civil lawsuit for the same crime. For example, a thief could be prosecuted by the state for breaking the law against stealing other people's property and could be sued by the owner of the property for violating the right of ownership. Similarly, if pharmacists dispense the wrong medication, then they could be prosecuted by the state for breaking the law against dispensing the wrong medication, and they could be sued by the patients for any damage the wrong drugs could have caused or benefits that were missed because the right drugs were not given. Breaking the law is a criminal law issue dealt with by the government; depriving people of their property or adversely affecting their health is a civil issue dealt with by the people involved (and their attorneys). Criminal issues almost always go to trial to determine guilt and punishment; civil issues almost never go to trial because the people involved (and their insurance companies) negotiate a settlement before the case gets to trial.

Malpractice

Malpractice is an issue of professional negligence. When pharmacists or technicians accidentally make mistakes through thoughtlessness or care-lessness, they are legally accountable for the consequences, and compensation is negotiated for and paid by the insurance companies that carry their professional insurance policies.

As with other types of civil cases, these rarely go to trial because settlements are almost always negotiated out of court. During the early part of the case, there may be preliminary motions in which the pharmacists or technicians try to have the case dismissed. This is called a *motion for summary judgment*. If the judge grants a motion for summary judgment, then the case is dismissed; if not, then it proceeds, and the negotiations for an out-of-court settlement become serious. Because most civil cases proceed to this point and then are settled, pretrial motions are where courts apply the law and create most of the precedents for others to follow in the future. In pharmacy cases, this means that courts' rulings on pretrial motions such as summary judgments are where they make most of the rulings that define the pharmacist's responsibilities. By allowing a case to proceed, the court is saying that the patient's complaint appears to be valid, and by granting the summary judgment and stopping the case, the court is saying that the pharmacist or technician appears to be in the right. The circumstances of the case are recorded and filed for future reference, adding to the body of common law just as an actual trial would. Of course, just like any other court action, these pretrial rulings can be appealed to a higher court.

The majority of malpractice cases involving pharmacists and technicians are simple dispensing errors: wrong drug, wrong strength, wrong label information, and so on. These types of errors should be addressed by the individual person's attentiveness to details as well as by the pharmacy's procedures. A well-run pharmacy has steps built into its dispensing procedure that make it more difficult to make a dispensing mistake. Things such as double checks by another person, a second form that requires data entry a second time, computer software that requires an additional check step or uses bar code technology to verify accuracy, and placement of inventory that prevents easily confused products from placement near each other even if the system would normally have them close together (e.g., cisplatin and carboplatin, both chemotherapy drugs, should be on entirely different shelving units even though they are close alphabetically). These are just a few basic concepts of risk management in medication safety. Having safety features in dispensing procedures makes it harder to make a mistake; counting solely on one person's attentiveness is a guarantee of failure. Dispensing errors are more of a system failure than a personnel problem.

Intellectual errors make up the rest of malpractice cases and are going to be increasingly significant with the introduction of more sophisticated drugs. Intellectual errors are those of judgment and information, for example, in confidentiality and patient counseling. Confidentiality is a basic responsibility of anyone with access to personal medical records, whether a drugstore's prescription file, a surgeon's report, or a psychiatrist's notes. We all need to be constantly aware of this and only look at information we need to see to do our jobs and then keep it to ourselves. Retail pharmacies are a particularly easy place for information to be misused in that we often need to discuss the filling or recording of a prescription, but the prescription counter is in a location where other people are easily within hearing. Retail pharmacy staff must be aware of this and keep such conversations in a low tone to avoid being overheard.

Patient counseling problems arise from lack of counseling, incomplete counseling, and wrong information. Patients have a right to be informed about their medications, and it is the pharmacist's duty to provide this information discretely and accurately. Many states allow this to be accomplished by patient information sheets dispensed with the medication; others require personal interaction. In 1990, the federal government passed a law called the Omnibus Budget Reconciliation Act of 1990, commonly called OBRA '90, which requires states to require medication counseling for all Medicaid patients unless these patients refuse it. Some states have made this counseling mandatory for all patients, and some have left it for only Medicaid patients, but it really does not matter in real practice. No pharmacist is going to take the time to look up a patient's Medicaid status and then decide to offer counseling or not, so in reality it affects all patients. OBRA '90 spells out what information must be given to a patient and instructs the states to develop ways of doing it. OBRA '90 is a good reference point for complaints about a failure to counsel or incomplete counseling. If a pharmacy provides accurate counseling that meets OBRA '90 standards and documents it, then it is doing the right thing for its patients, and it can prove it if a question arises in the future. Patient counseling is a time-consuming duty, but it is just that: a duty. A pharmacy technician's role is to know when to turn the patient over to the pharmacist for information and to support the pharmacist's counseling efforts.

Almost all pharmacy malpractice cases are the result of unintentional mistakes that all humans make even if they are trying to do their best; the mistakes are rarely intentional or the result of sheer thoughtlessness or irresponsible actions. The question then arises regarding whether a person should be liable for a simple, unintentional mistake. Surely, if great harm was done, then someone has to take responsibility regardless of whether it was accidental, but what if there was no great harm? The law allows for this by requiring three things to be present for something to be professional negligence:

1. A breach of duty occurred.
2. Damages are significant.
3. The professional's action or inaction is the direct cause.

If any one of these three is missing, then it was a simple mistake, and no legal liability exists.

A *breach of duty* occurs when something is expected of a person in a position of responsibility, and it is not provided. The duty of pharmacy personnel is one of a high degree of care, in fact requiring virtually an error-free standard. Pharmacists are expected to provide the right thing to the right person in the right way every time, which is an impossible expectation. However, this is made workable by the doctrine of a "reasonable and prudent person." That is, a pharmacist or technician is expected to do what a reasonable and prudent person would have done under similar circumstances. It is easy to criticize and second-guess someone's actions with the benefit of hindsight, so the courts will attempt to determine what a competent professional person should have done at the time by calling expert witnesses to give their opinions. If the professional's actions were reasonable and prudent given the circumstances, then the duty was fulfilled appropriately. This is no excuse for carelessness or thoughtlessness because human fallibility is not a defense, but if the work is carried out thoughtfully and carefully in a manner that was intended to be in the patient's best interest, then the pharmacist is doing the right thing.

To be able to legally claim negligence, the patient must have been harmed — no harm, no malpractice. It becomes less clear when we try to define *harm*. Physical harm is quite clear in that the person would have had some kind of medical reaction to the error and should be compensated for lost wages, if any. It should be easy to determine a dollar value for that, but it becomes an issue when compensation is for illness, injury, pain, or emotional stress because calculation of value is difficult for all. In such cases, a jury will award money to make the harm that was done somewhat easier to tolerate. The pain or emotional distress will probably still be there, but a financial award attempts to make dealing with it easier. If the error was particularly significant or the pharmacy personnel did not do the reasonable-and-prudent thing, then money for punitive damages may also be awarded to make an example of them and to punish them.

The third factor is one of cause: did the pharmacist's action or inaction cause the harm? This can be difficult to determine. If there is disagreement over which drug was dispensed and used, then the evidence has long ago been eliminated from the person's body, making it difficult for the patient to prove anything. If the medicine is known, then there may be a question of whether something else, other than the medicine, might have caused the harm. Another factor is whether the patient took action to treat the problem; for example, if a person receives too high a strength of digoxin from the pharmacy and notices adverse effects, then it would be within a day or two of starting to take the higher strength. If the patient immediately calls the doctor about these effects, then a good case could be made against the pharmacy, but if 2 weeks are allowed to elapse, the court may find that the plaintiff's inaction caused much of the problem, and the pharmacy's liability will be far lower. Another question is one of involvement of other people's actions or inactions; that is, did someone else do something that was the true cause of the problem? For example, pharmacy personnel may have committed a breach of duty by not warning a patient to keep medicine away from children, but the pharmacy can hardly be held accountable for something that happens if a grandparent thoughtlessly leaves an open prescription vial on a low table where a toddler can reach it. The pharmacy's failure to warn may have been a contributing factor, but the grandparent's negligence is the true cause, and in this case, the pharmacy's liability will be either minimal or none at all.

Laws are a system of rules used to control the actions of people. These rules of conduct are formally considered to be binding and are enforced by a recognized authority to provide security and safety for society. When someone disobeys or "breaks" a law, a penalty is handed down by a court. These penalties, which are written into the law, vary depending on the severity of the crime committed. For this reason in particular, professionals in the medical field carry liability insurance. Like other insurance, liability insurance carries one main objective or purpose — to spread the risk of loss among all the members who carry the same insurance.

Medical professionals, including pharmacists and pharmacy technicians, wish to protect their assets. In case of a judgment against these professionals, liability insurance will help defray their out-of-pocket losses and costs. Each member pays a premium that is pooled and drawn from if members have claims charged against them. Whenever a health care professional deals with others, a chance exists that something can unintentionally go wrong. It is important for such professionals to protect not only their assets, but also themselves. Liability insurance is a must. Luckily, it is also relatively inexpensive.

Although the obvious risk of loss is that of a judgment or penalty imposed for malpractice, another risk factor lessened by insurance is that of defending oneself even if innocent. Often, many people are drawn into a lawsuit when they really are not the targets; yet, they are forced to hire lawyers to defend themselves and, hopefully, have the case dismissed. Professional liability insurance deals with this issue, making defense affordable.

SAMPLE QUESTIONS FOR STUDENT REVIEW

1. Which three government entities together create laws, and how are they applied?
2. What is enabling legislation?
3. Which three factors determine whether a regulation is legal?
4. Where would a listing of all finalized federal regulations be found?
5. Who has the final say on what a law really means?
6. What is the difference between criminal and civil law?
7. What is a tort?
8. What is a contract?
9. What is a motion for summary judgment?
10. Most malpractice cases involve which type of error?
11. Are most dispensing errors caused by human error or dispensing system flaws?
12. What legislation spells out the information that should be given to a patient for adequate counseling?
13. Which three things must occur before a mistake is considered negligence? Define each of them.

2

HISTORY AND DEVELOPMENT
OF CURRENT LAW

OVERVIEW AND OBJECTIVES

Early laws regarding prescription drugs in the United States were essentially nonexistent, which led to frightening incidents and public outcry for protection by the government. As a result, the rule of law regarding prescription drugs in America was quickly updated in the early to mid-1900s and was soon the model of the developed world. Because of the strength of states' rights in our system of government, both the federal government and individual states have laws and regulations controlling prescription drugs and their uses. Although both address many of the same subjects, the federal government has more say in some areas, and in others, the states have more influence.

Chapter 2 discusses the following subjects:

- Early lack of government oversight
- Foreign involvement in drug distribution
- Several developments leading to legislation that affects us today
- Which topics are dealt with by the federal government
- Which topics are dealt with by the state governments
- How state and federal governments handle topics with which both deal
- Roles of state and federal governments

The federal government controls drugs through two major laws, the federal Food, Drug, and Cosmetic Act (FDCA) and the federal Controlled Substances Act (CSA), which are discussed in Chapters 3 and 4.

The FDCA is mostly concerned with regulating the manufacturing, distribution, sale, prescribing, storage, record keeping, and dispensing of drugs. This is handled by the Food and Drug Administration (FDA), a branch of the Department of Health and Human Services. The CSA deals only with those drugs that have addictive potential and can be abused. These drugs, called *controlled substances*, are monitored by special regulations regarding record keeping and registration of those who handle them. A branch of the Federal Bureau of Investigation called the Drug Enforcement Administration (DEA) administers the CSA. Because there is quite a bit of overlap in their responsibilities, the FDA and DEA cooperate in their efforts; for example, the DEA gets scientific advice from the FDA when it is deciding which drugs to include in its controlled substances lists.

State rules and regulations have their greatest role in the area of licensing and dispensing. The states decide what kind of licenses are necessary for prescribers, pharmacists, pharmacy technicians, and pharmacies, as well as what requirements must be met before they can be issued. States also have more requirements for prescription dispensing than the federal government does. Consequently, much of what pharmacists do while dispensing prescriptions is a result of state requirements. Students reading chapters on federal law should keep in mind that their own state laws and board of pharmacy regulations will be much more extensive. While taking an exam on federal law or taking the Pharmacy Technician Certification Board (PTCB) certification exam, they will need to remember what comes from federal requirements and what is added by a particular state.

Each state has its own FDCA and CSA legislation, most of which simply copy the federal laws to the point of even using the exact wording of the FDCA and CSA. When the federal and state laws deal with the same subject but do not exactly agree with each other, the stricter rule is the one that will apply; for example, if federal law specifies that certain records must be stored for 3 years but state law specifies 5 years, then everyone in that state must keep records for 5 years.

INTO THE 20TH CENTURY

Lack of Controls

While the United States was a young, developing nation, issues such as regulating the few drugs in existence were not considered important. Europe and other nations had realized the importance of such regulations and were far ahead of the United States, which resulted in some unique and interesting developments in the late 1800s and early 1900s. Many people and businesses took advantage of the lack of government involvement and the innocence of the general public.

In the United States before the 20th century, the regulation of the sale of drugs was practically nonexistent. Opium, morphine, and cocaine, all opiate drugs with high abuse potential, were both legally and readily available without prescription. These medications, mixed with a high percentage of alcohol, were quite often ingredients in the "miracle cure" syrups, elixirs, and potions found in pharmacies, general stores, catalogs, and traveling medicine shows. Traveling salesmen calling themselves "Doctor" would sell bottles of the miracle elixir for $1 apiece and then move quickly on to the next town before their deception was uncovered. Pharmacies and other retail businesses would brew up whatever concoctions they wished and sell them alongside legitimate manufactured medications and local traditional remedies. Claims were made that these so-called miracle cures could heal anything from sprains and fevers to gout and tuberculosis and, in fact, usually did make people feel better, but not because of any therapeutic benefit. The opiates and alcohol simply reduced pain and produced a euphoric state.

In addition, this lack of oversight resulted in products that were contaminated with various chemicals as well as insect parts and rodent hair and droppings. Many people became ill because of this chemical and animal contamination.

At the time, no law required manufacturers actually to state the contents of their products, so often no ingredients at all were listed on the product's label. In addition, wild claims could be made regarding the product's usefulness without fear of legal action.

Laws and regulations are usually a result of some event that prompts lawmakers and regulators to react in response. When a problem develops and people are hurt or money is lost, a new law or regulation comes about to address the problem. There are some occasions when government action is taken to head off a possible problem, but that is relatively unusual.

Foreign Manufacturers' Influence

Although European countries had laws and restrictions regarding drug composition, the United States lacked the laws and regulations that would ensure drug quality and purity. Because of the absence of these laws, the United States became the world's dumping ground for substandard, contaminated, and often dangerous drugs. When a European manufacturer had problems with quality control regulations in its own country, it would simply sell the problem batch to an American company, which would then distribute it in the United States without government interference.

Early Misbranding of Miracle Cures

Because both the safety and efficacy of many products available in the 1800s and early 1900s were unknown, and because of the numerous reports of people becoming addicted to the opiates and alcohol as well as being hurt by contamination, Dr. Harvey Wiley, a physician and congressman, persuaded congress to pass the Federal Food and Drug Act of 1906, commonly called the Wiley Act of 1906.

This act banned adulterated and misbranded food, drink, and drugs from interstate commerce. Although with the passing of this act the need for regulation was finally recognized, this law was ultimately considered inadequate for a number of reasons:

■ Untrue statements made by the manufacturer were not considered misbranding by the courts.

■ This act included legislation regarding only food, drink, and drugs, not cosmetics.

■ Although this act limited commerce to those drugs that were safe, it did not authorize the banning of unsafe drugs.

■ Finally, the medication's contents were still not required to be identified on labels.

Congress corrected the false statement situation by including a definition of misbranding that encompassed "false or fraudulent claims," but other problems were not addressed. Of course, this left consumers almost as unprotected as before, so the Wiley Act of 1906 did not accomplish much other than being the first time it was recognized that drugs and other consumables needed regulation to protect the public.

Opium and Heroin "Epidemic" of the Early 1900s

By the early 1900s, it was a widely recognized fact that narcotic drugs possessed a high potential for abuse, and "opium dens," where people smoked opium and its chemical derivatives, were commonplace in metropolitan areas worldwide. President Teddy Roosevelt referred to opium as the greatest threat to the safety of the United States at that time.

In an attempt to control this class of drugs, the International Opium Convention of 1912 was held at The Hague in The Netherlands. Numerous nations came together with the hopes of controlling narcotics through international agreements and treaties. Each nation that signed the agreement was to designate specific ports and towns where raw opium could be legally imported and exported. In addition, only persons specifically licensed could import or export opium. Importation or exportation of opium used for smoking, also called *prepared opium*, was prohibited. The nations also decided to limit the manufacture of morphine, cocaine, and similar chemicals. The establishments where these drugs could be manufactured, sold, or exported had to be licensed to do so, and persons who were registered to import or export these compounds were required to keep up-to-date records of the amounts handled. The use of these drugs was then limited to legitimate and medical uses only. Finally, the import and export of these narcotic drugs were to be supervised by each government.

To fulfill these provisions, the U.S. Congress adopted the Federal Narcotic Drug Act in 1914, also called the Harrison Narcotic Act of 1914, after its primary sponsor. This act attempted to control narcotic drugs by mandating that containers must exhibit a tax stamp. The importer or manufacturer of the narcotic drug was required to purchase governmental tax stamps and seal the narcotic drug container with such a stamp, which verified that it had entered the marketplace through proper channels.

Under this act and its following amendments, it was unlawful to either sell or possess narcotics unless they were in an original stamped package. Two exceptions to this rule were observed. The first allowed a person to possess narcotics without a tax stamp if the narcotics were obtained through a legal written prescription issued for a legitimate medical purpose. Instead of the tax stamp, the container had to bear the name and registry number of the pharmacist and the prescriber as well as the name and address of the patient. Refills of these prescriptions were not allowed. The second exception allowed patients to possess a container free of a tax stamp if the narcotic was lawfully administered or provided by a licensed prescriber. This was the first time the concepts of a prescription and a prescriber appeared in the law.

Sulfanilamide Disaster of 1937

Sulfanilamide was a widely used topical anti-infective. It was thought to be a miracle drug because it was by far the most effective product in fighting infections in wounds and cuts. In World War I and early World War II, military medics on the battlefield would cover a wound with this yellow, sulfur-based powder and dress the area with clean bandages as the standard treatment, resulting in a huge decrease in combat deaths from infected wounds. Prior to this, infection was the main cause of death of wounded soldiers, not blood loss or the damage caused by the actual wound itself.

In 1937, a manufacturer decided to market a liquid form of the drug to be used to treat sore throats. The sulfanilamide was mixed with diethylene glycol, a light pink, sweet-tasting liquid that would mask the taste of the sulfanilamide. Unfortunately, no clinical tests were required or conducted before the product was marketed. As we now realize, diethylene glycol — or what is more commonly known today as automobile antifreeze — is a highly poisonous substance. There were 107 reported deaths caused by the ingestion of the mixture, and the manufacturer was prosecuted by the FDA for manufacturing and marketing an untested, unapproved product. Pharmaceutical organizations came to the manufacturer's defense, pointing out that laws and regulations in this area were inadequate and incomplete in that the FDA did not have the authority to ban unsafe drugs (ultimately, the manufacturer was prosecuted for misbranding because the medicine was labeled as an elixir but contained no alcohol; the definition of an elixir is that it contains alcohol). New legislation was passed within a year, the sweeping federal Food, Drug, and Cosmetics Act of 1938, which is addressed in Chapter 3.

Increasing Sophistication and Complexity of New Drugs

With the discovery and marketing of penicillin in the 1940s, research and development of new drugs increased dramatically, resulting in many products that were too sophisticated and complicated for the average person to understand and use safely and properly. The original legislation required all products to be labeled as we see over-the-counter (OTC) drugs labeled today, and many new drugs were just too complex or potentially dangerous for the general public to be able to choose and use them wisely. The realization of this produced an amendment to the FDCA, the Durham-Humphrey Amendment of 1952. This separated drugs into those that could be properly handled by an average person after reading the label and package information and those that could not. The second were called *prescription drugs* and could only be sold or used under the supervision of a prescriber, who would choose the product and monitor its use.

This finally created the broad categories of OTC and prescription drugs with which we are familiar today, with their different labeling and professional supervision requirements. Those now listed in the new prescription drugs category could be obtained only through the authorization of a supervising prescriber and needed to be labeled with only comparatively little information. All new drugs were ordered to be prescription drugs until it was proven that they could be properly and safely used by the general public without a prescriber's supervision. Also included were drugs that were deemed to be habit forming and those that were not safe for self-medication because of toxicity, potentiality for harmful effect, or complexity of use. Prescription drug containers had to be labeled with the statement "Caution: Federal law prohibits dispensing without a prescription"; they are sometimes called *legend* drugs because this statement, or legend, is required.

Thalidomide Disaster of 1962

In 1962, a sleeping pill and antiemetic named thalidomide was under study in the United States. It had been widely used worldwide to treat nausea in the first trimester of pregnancy, but it was not yet approved for use in the United States. While investigating the use of the drug, the William S. Merrell Company of Cincinnati discovered that the drug could harm a fetus if the mother took thalidomide during the first trimester because, in western Europe, the drug had been associated with thousands of deformed babies. The malformation was that the babies were born either without arms or with severely deformed limbs, a deformity known as *phocomelia*. Dr. Frances O. Kelsey, a physician working for the FDA, was instrumental in keeping thalidomide off the U.S. market. Unfortunately, many babies with phocomelia were born to American women who had taken or purchased thalidomide when abroad.

The public became concerned about just how much was known about drugs before they were introduced into the marketplace, and Senator Estes Kefauver led Senate committee hearings on the issue of premarket research and safety and effectiveness of drugs. This became a huge media event after a Texas woman who had taken thalidomide during the first trimester of a pregnancy traveled to Europe to obtain an abortion out of fear of bearing a deformed child (abortions were difficult to obtain in the United States at that time). Her decision, as well as the controversy over inadequate and sometimes falsified premarket testing, were the subjects of magazine cover stories, segments on network news shows, and sermons in churches across the country.

People became nervous about drugs in general, and it was obvious that new legislation was needed. The answer was the 1962 Kefauver-Harris Amendment, which required manufacturers to prove the effectiveness of their products before marketing them. Safety issues were also expanded from what previous legislation had required, and several requirements for good manufacturing practices, such as those regarding cleanliness, storage, and purity, were put in place. In addition, better procedures for new drug investigations and approval applications were initiated.

Habit-Forming and Dangerous Drugs

Society became more alert to the dangers of some drugs through a consensus based not on specific instances, such as mentioned in this chapter, but on an awareness that developed gradually. Street use of heroin and other chemicals, the emergence of gangs in urban centers and their trafficking in these items, and the dangers to individuals and society that were presented in these conditions led lawmakers to move to control these dangerous substances. In 1970, the Federal Comprehensive Drug Abuse Prevention and Control Act of 1970, usually called the Controlled Substances Act (CSA), was passed. This legislation, which created methods of controlling drugs that were deemed dangerous through their potential for abuse and addiction, is discussed in Chapter 4.

SAMPLE QUESTIONS FOR STUDENT REVIEW

1. What is the FDA?
2. What is the DEA?
3. Which has the most influence in licensing and dispensing practices, individual states or the federal government?
4. Describe the status of drug laws in the United States in the 1800s.
5. What was the first drug control law in the United States?
6. What was the main focus of the Durham-Humphrey Amendment to the FDCA?
7. What is the difference between the labeling requirements for OTC and prescription drugs?

3

FOOD, DRUG, AND COSMETIC ACT OF 1938

OVERVIEW AND OBJECTIVES

The Federal Food, Drug, and Cosmetic Act (FDCA) of 1938, as described in Chapter 2, was formulated as a reaction to instances that occurred because of lack of governmental controls. Although people do not want governments to control their lives more than necessary, there are certain things that can be done only by government actions. Protecting each citizen from adulterated or misbranded drugs is one of those things; no one person has the ability or resources to make such determinations independently, so the FDCA and its amendments are meant to provide this protection through the actions of the Food and Drug Administration (FDA) as it administers the FDCA.

Chapter 3 discusses the following subjects:

- Adulteration and misbranding
- Prohibited acts
- Handling of samples
- Testing and introducing new drugs
- Prescribing and dispensing

ADULTERATION

To *adulterate* something is to make it impure or inferior by using or adding the wrong ingredients. The FDCA is interestingly descriptive in this in saying, "if it consists in whole or in part of any filthy, putrid, or decomposed substance." This part of the legislation does not deal with the actual purity or quality of the final drug product; for example, a substance used to give bulk to a tablet may decompose slightly without harming the product or a person who uses it, but the product would still be adulterated. And, just what is "filthy" or "putrid" and when would a drug product affected by either become a health hazard or have its quality or purity affected? The FDA has several regulations that clear up such definitions, but affecting the quality or purity of a product is not necessary to have violated the FDCA; the mere presence of filthy, putrid, or decomposed material is a violation even if the presence is not enough to make a difference. This of course applies to the manufacturing process, something that retail, hospital, or investigational pharmacies would rarely, if ever, be involved in, but something of a daily concern to manufacturers and distributors.

Another statement says that if a product is prepared or held under unsanitary conditions by which it may have been contaminated with filth or otherwise have become possibly injurious to a person's health or if the facilities or procedures did not meet current good manufacturing practices, then it is an adulterated product. Again, no reference is made to the actual quality or purity of the product in these statements. A product is considered adulterated if the conditions at the factory, or during shipping or storage, were not up to standards, regardless of whether the product itself was affected. This applies to all aspects of pharmacy and drug manufacturing and distribution. Good manufacturing practices are explained in the regulations governing manufacturers, and their facilities must meet them or be considered to be breaking the law. The word *held* makes this segment apply to shipping companies, wholesalers, and all pharmacies in that the methods of handling and storing drugs must meet certain standards. A retail or hospital pharmacy must keep its storage areas clean and under controlled temperatures, refrigeration must be used when called for, products must be stored on shelves off the floor, and other considerations must be met to satisfy the requirements for proper storage. Samples of the drugs are an issue here because a salesperson might transport them in the trunk of an automobile, where it may be unclean and the temperature uncontrolled.

A product is considered adulterated if the container is made of a substance that might affect the drug inside. There are standards explaining the type and quality of the glass or plastic used in drug containers, both bulk containers from the manufacturer or distributor and the individual prescription vials in which the drugs are dispensed to consumers. The right type of plastic or glass will prevent outside substances from leaching into the vial and contaminating the drugs inside and will also prevent the drug product from vaporizing or leaching out of the vial, which would reduce its strength. This is why nitroglycerin sublingual tablets must be in a certain type of glass vial rather than plastic; no plastic can prevent it from vaporizing, so some of the drug would escape, and the tablets would not stay up to strength if a plastic vial were used.

A separate statement in the FDCA refers to the requirement that strength, quality, and purity must be up to the claims made on the label.

MISBRANDING

The term *misbranding* is somewhat self-explanatory in that it deals with the label statements on the bulk container and on the prescription vial. The first and main provision of this section is so broad that it seems to cover just about any situation. It states that a drug is misbranded if its label is false or misleading in any way. This phrasing applies not only when a prescription drug is dispensed without there being an active prescription (perhaps there are no refills left, or perhaps it is just sold illegally without a prescription), but also any time the bulk container label misrepresents the product (such as in the case of imitation or counterfeit drugs) or does not list all ingredients, either active and inactive.

Over-the-counter (OTC) medication labels must contain adequate directions for use and adequate warnings against use to allow the average person to use a drug safely and for the intended purpose. An extensive list exists of exactly what must be included on the OTC label to meet this requirement, and the FDA must approve a label before the product can be marketed. The first part of this is commonly called the seven-point label, which consists of

1. Approved name of the drug
2. Name and address of the manufacturer or distributor
3. Amount contained in the package
4. Approved names of all active and inactive ingredients
5. Name of any habit-forming component
6. Cautions and warnings for the consumer
7. Adequate directions for use

Several other points must also be included:

- Intended conditions and purposes
- Normal dose for each intended use and for people of different ages and physical conditions
- Frequency and duration of administration
- Administration related to meals, symptoms, or other time factors
- Route or method of administration
- Any necessary preparations for use (such as mixing in water, etc.)

The label of a prescription drug bulk container as it is purchased from the manufacturer or wholesaler has its own set of requirements meant to supply adequate information for use for the practitioner rather than the patient and contains the scientific and medical information needed to aid in its appropriate prescription. Because this information is so extensive, it is usually provided by means of an informational insert packaged into the bulk container or glued to it. This insert must contain the following topics in the order listed (this uniform order helps people look up specific topics quickly because they are always presented in the same sequence):

- Chemical and physical description
- Clinical pharmacology
- Indications and usage
- Contraindications
- Warnings
- Precautions
- Adverse reactions
- Drug abuse and dependence
- Overdosage topics
- Dosage and administration
- How supplied (product description and packaging)
- Date of label revision

In addition, several other points must appear on the outer label of the container:

- Name and address of the manufacturer or distributor
- Approved name of the drug
- Quantity and amount of each active ingredient
- Quantity of each unit (that is, the strength of each tablet, etc., e.g., "100 mg")
- Total units in the container (e.g., "500 tablets")
- Usual dosage or a statement referring the reader to the package insert
- The symbol "Rx Only" or the legend "Caution: Federal law prohibits dispensing without a prescription"
- Route of administration if anything other than for oral use
- Lot number
- Statement telling the pharmacy what type of container in which to dispense the prescription
- Expiration date, if applicable (a few products do not have expiration dates, mostly things used in compounding)

An additional component of the bulk container's label is the National Drug Code (NDC) number. The NDC number is unique for each product and package size and is 11 digits long: the first 5 digits identify the manufacturer or distributor; the next 4 digits identify the product name, strength, and dosage form; and the last 2 digits refer to the package size. This information is useful in inventory control as well as in conjunction with electronic dispensing records, such as seen with bar code checking.

DRUG SAMPLES

Drug samples are intended only to promote the sale of the drug. Although many patients benefit from receiving these "free" samples, the manufacturer's purpose is simply to get the prescriber to use the product and therefore influence prescribing habits. Once prescribers become familiar and comfortable with a drug, they tend to continue using it (writing prescriptions for it) after the supply of samples is gone.

Although this may seem to benefit the patients who receive these free samples, many problems can arise. One is that no pharmacy has a record of the drug's use in the patient's profile. This can be dangerous in that drug–drug interactions and drug allergies will be missed by the pharmacy's checking system, with potentially dangerous consequences. Another is that most patients see several physicians, which leaves the pharmacy as the only source of complete drug records on a patient; samples would not be included in the pharmacy's records. In addition, samples are not usually kept under ideal storage conditions by the salespeople distributing them, which might affect the expiration date of the product as well as its cleanliness.

Drug samples may not be legally sold or traded, but because no records have historically been kept on them, they presented a great temptation; many prescribers sold or traded them to pharmacies, which then repackaged and dispensed them. While repackaging, the drugs would be removed from their original packaging and mingled with other lot numbers, breaking misbranding and adulteration rules. A 1987 amendment to drug sample regulations sought to better regulate this activity. Before this amendment, unsolicited samples were mailed directly to physicians, with individual prescribers often receiving many each day. These were not always related to the prescriber's field of practice, which led to more of the sale and trading mentioned. The 1987 amendment now requires a written request before a sample can be provided either directly by the manufacturer or distributor or personally by the sales representative. This request must list several details, such as the name and quantity of the drug, the manufacturer, and the requesting physician's name. A receipt must also be signed by the physician and kept by the manufacturer or distributor for at least 3 years. The prescriber may ask to receive the samples personally or may designate another health care provider or hospital pharmacy to receive them. If representatives from the manufacturer distribute them, then an annual inventory must be taken to determine where the samples are stored. If drug samples are stolen, misplaced, or unaccountable, then these instances must be reported to the Secretary of Health and Human Services.

INVESTIGATIONAL NEW DRUGS

Definition

It is generally recognized that the FDA's greatest role is to decide and regulate which drugs will be made commercially available in the United States. Before any new drug may be commercially sold, imported, or transported between states, it must first be approved by the FDA. This is controlled by the filing and approval of two forms: the Investigational New Drug (IND) form and the New Drug Application (NDA).

Perhaps before discussing new drug approvals, what a "drug" is, according to the FDCA, should be defined. A substance is considered a *drug* when one of these factors applies to it:

- It is a substance recognized in one of the three official reference books for the chemicals used as drug products. These are the *United States Pharmacopeia*, often just called the USP, which deals primarily with the chemical specifications of a drug; the *National Formulary*, often just called the NF, which deals primarily with use and application of a drug; or the *Homeopathic Pharmacopeia of the United States*, which deals only with homeopathic remedies and treatments.
- It is something intended for use "in the diagnosis, cure, mitigation, treatment or prevention of disease in man or other animals."
- It is something other than food intended to affect the structure or any function of the body of humans or other animals.
- It is something used as a component of anything in the above three categories.

Now, we can move on to what is considered a *new drug*. The full text of the FDCA's definition of a new drug is as follows:

- Any drug (except a new animal drug or animal feed bearing or containing a new animal drug) the composition of which is such that such drug is not generally recognized among experts qualified by scientific training and experience to evaluate the safety and effectiveness of drugs, as safe and effective for use under the conditions prescribed, recommended, or suggested in the labeling thereof, except that such a drug not so recognized shall not be deemed a "new drug" if, at any time prior to June 25, 1938, it was subject to the Food and Drug Act of June 30, 1906, as amended and if at such time its labeling contained the same representations concerning the conditions of its use; or

■ Any drug (except a new animal drug or an animal feed bearing or containing a new animal drug) the composition of which is such that such drug, as a result of investigations to determine its safety and effectiveness for use under such conditions, has become so recognized, but which has not, otherwise in such investigations, been used to material extent or for a material time under such conditions.

What this means is that a drug "becomes a new drug" and must follow new drug application procedures when

■ A substance that composes such a drug, whether an active substance, carrier, or coating, is new for drug use. This means that if a change is made in the coating, the ink used on the tablet or capsule, the binding or filler materials used to make the bulk of the tablet or to fill a capsule, or any other part of the product, a new form must be filed to get approval.

■ Two or more substances, neither of which is a new drug, are combined for drug use. In this case, if a manufacturer wants to make a new combination product using drugs that had already been approved as individual products, a new form must be filed to get approval.

■ There is a change in the proportions of a combination of substances for drug use. That is, if any change is made in the amounts of any drug in an already approved combination product, a new form must be filed.

■ A new use for a drug is claimed even though the drug is not new when used in the treatment of another disease; that is, an addition to the listed indications for drug use. IND and NDA forms specify what the product is to be used for. If a manufacturer wants to add another use or change the currently approved use, a new form must be filed.

■ A new dosage, method, or duration of application is recommended or suggested. Any change in any of these requires a new form to be filed.

Only one exception to these rules is recognized. Some drugs were exempt from the new drug procedures because they had been in general use for a very long time (since prior to 1938, when the FDCA was passed). It was thought that any problems with drugs in general use that long were well known already, so further studies were unnecessary. However, these drugs are exempt only if the claims and representations on their labels have remained the same. If any of these drugs vary in chemistry, strength, route of administration, dosage, or indication for use, then these "new versions" must comply with new drug procedures.

Procedures

Studies conducted by computer modeling and on laboratory animals are undertaken before an IND or NDA is filed. If the manufacturer then concludes that the drug investigated may be beneficial in treating a certain disease or medical problem, then the manufacturer will then file an IND with the FDA. This filing indicates that the computer and animal studies have convinced the researchers that the investigational drug should be relatively safe to administer during trials using human subjects.

According to FDA regulation 21 C.F.R. 312, an IND must contain

- A description of the composition of the drug and methods of manufacture.
- A statement of methods of manufacture and quality control.
- A statement of all information derived from earlier investigations, including identification and qualifications of the investigators and enough information to allow scientific review of the sponsor's conclusions.
- A statement about the drug's history, copies of information supplied to the investigator, including all relevant hazards and the identities and experience of each clinical investigator.
- An outline of the proposed phases of the investigation, which is usually conducted in three phases. In Phase 1, the drug is given to people only in small amounts with the purpose of determining toxicity, safe dosage range, metabolism, absorption, and elimination. Phase 1 involves only a few dozen human subjects. Phase 2 covers initial trials on a limited number of persons for the control or prevention of a specific disease. This usually involves a few hundred human subjects. Phase 3 covers the final testing of the drug for safety, effectiveness, and dosages on a large number of patients already affected by the disease or on research subjects, usually numbering several hundred to several thousand human subjects.

■ A statement identifying an institutional review board with continuing reviewing authority over the investigations. Any institution (a hospital or university, for example) that does investigational studies on humans must have an institutional review board that oversees these investigations to be sure all regulations are followed. This is important for patient safety as well as for the quality of the studies.

■ An agreement by the sponsor to report any significant hazards, contraindications, side effects encountered, or adverse drug experiences during the investigation.

Studies on humans may not begin until 30 days after the FDA receives the IND notice.

An IND's purpose is to tell the FDA about the investigation and its protocol and procedures to ensure the quality of the investigation. Patients' and investigational subjects' rights are also outlined in the protocol. An IND only notifies the FDA of the investigation; this does not imply an official endorsement of the investigation by the FDA.

The investigational drug must be labeled with the legend "Caution: New drug: Limited by federal law to investigational use" and is usually handled only by hospital or research pharmacies, although clinic pharmacies may occasionally be involved.

Because of the potential commercial value of a new drug, the FDA does not disclose any information about an IND except to human subjects who receive the investigational drug. The FDA believes these individuals have the right to know about any adverse reactions that have arisen during animal studies or earlier phases of human studies. The people involved must be informed of all aspects of the drug and its investigation, and they must sign a form indicating what they were told and that they understand it; copies of this form are kept in the patient's medical record as well as by the investigating physician and the manufacturer or research institution.

Only investigators named in the protocol of the investigational drugs may prescribe them. They may not be prescribed by any other physician.

NEW DRUG APPLICATIONS

Definition

After a drug company successfully completes an IND and determines that the drug is both safe and effective for the indicated purpose, the company then files an NDA with the FDA. This procedure is the main regulatory device the FDA uses to control drugs in the United States.

Procedures

Contained in the NDA submitted by the drug's sponsor is basically all of the information it has about the drug. Included are all references to any other investigational new drugs affecting the drug, methods of manufacture, evaluation of safety and effectiveness, chemistry, names of investigators and their full reports, and both proposed labeling of the drug and proposed instructions regarding how it is to be prescribed.

After the NDA is complete, the FDA will review the application. If the FDA feels that more information is needed, then the sponsor will have to respond with the requested additional information. Then, "if the application is supported by substantial evidence that the drug will have the effect it purports or is represented to have under the conditions of use prescribed or suggested in the labeling," the NDA is approved. That is, if the FDA review committee agrees with the study's conclusions as stated in the NDA, then the company is permitted to go ahead and market the product.

Postmarketing Adverse Reaction Reporting

Just because an NDA is approved does not mean the sponsor's responsibilities have ended. The sponsor must maintain a system of records and make periodic reports to the FDA regarding the drug. These reports are made numerous times annually for many years.

Even though a newly approved drug has undergone extensive study and testing, once it is commercially available to the general population the drug is used by many more people than it was while the studies were ongoing. Because of this increased use, the potential for the appearance of adverse drug reactions is greater. The FDA requires that any information about adverse drug effects, injury, drug toxicity, or other unexpected adverse events be reported with 15 days of the adverse event.

Health care professionals are learning to recognize potential drug safety problems associated with drug therapy. The FDA has started a program to encourage all health care workers to directly report all adverse drug reactions to the FDA. Serious adverse drug reactions include hospitalization, severe disability, and death. Even if the adverse drug reaction is not severe, the FDA encourages health care professionals to report all adverse reactions — even those potential reactions that are included in the drug information. After a report is filed, the FDA adheres to the policy of complete confidentiality. Neither the professional reporting the reaction nor the patient's identity will be disclosed.

The Drug Price Competition and Patent-Term Restoration Act of 1984

The introduction of generic drugs engendered intense competition between generic manufacturers and manufacturers of innovative or "pioneer" drugs. This led to legislation, the Drug Price Competition and Patent-Term Restoration Act of 1984, intended to encourage both the introduction of generic copies of pioneer drugs and the continuing research and innovation that leads to new drug concepts and therapies. This legislation gives advantages to both types of manufacturers, with the public the ultimate winner by having cheaper generic copies available while still enjoying the benefits of new products.

This legislation allows generic manufacturers to introduce a product without going through the IND and NDA research and approval process, thereby shaving years and cost from the introduction of the generic product. The generic manufacturer files an Abbreviated New Drug Application (ANDA), through which the only studies that must be conducted are human studies on the bioavailability (that is, the drug's absorption and distribution characteristics) and bioequivalence (that is, how closely its effects mimic the original pioneer drug). This lower cost and shorter time encourage the introduction of generic products, which saves money for consumers, government programs, and insurance companies but could take market share and resultant profits from the innovating manufacturer. To compensate for this potential loss, the legislation allows the FDA to grant extensions to the exclusive marketing time that patents provide. Generally, a patent gives an innovator 17 years in which to be the only company allowed to sell and profit from a patented product. Because patents are granted long before the IND and NDA research process is over, innovating manufacturers enjoy patent protection from competition for much less than this 17 years; this act allows the FDA to extend this for 2 to 5 years when a competing generic product is proposed. This extended exclusive marketing period is intended to compensate the innovator for the studies required by IND and NDA processes that the generic manufacturer did not need to carry out.

THE ORPHAN DRUG ACT OF 1983

The IND and NDA procedures are time consuming and expensive, so manufacturers will pursue only those drugs that they feel will generate enough sales volume to cover these expenses and still turn a profit. Unfortunately, this means that drugs to treat diseases affecting only a few people will not be developed and marketed; products must generate profits to enable the manufacturer to stay in business, and if there are not enough people who need a certain drug, its manufacture will not be profitable. Congress responded to this issue by passing the Orphan Drug Act of 1983, which gives tax incentives and enhanced marketing rights to manufacturers who develop these drugs. Such drugs are routinely called *orphan drugs*.

The downside of this seemingly noble idea is that there have been cases of a manufacturer's initially requesting FDA approval of a drug as an orphan drug when actually it may have other uses that are more widespread. Then, once it has gained orphan drug tax and licensing advantages, the manufacturer sponsors researchers who publish articles about the other uses in more common diseases (see the section on approved versus unapproved uses). This then gives the manufacturer the tax and marketing advantages of an orphan drug while enjoying the profits of its other, more-widespread use. Thankfully, such unethical behavior is not a common occurrence.

PRESCRIBING REQUIREMENTS AND RESTRICTIONS

Who May Prescribe Prescription Drugs (see also Appendix 8)

Although the federal government plays an important role in drug regulation, the individual states have the power to regulate the terms and conditions for obtaining and holding a license. State governments have the authority to determine who can practice as a physician, pharmacist, dentist, nurse, and the like and determines what a health care provider can legally do. This is referred to as *scope of practice*. For example, podiatrists, or foot doctors, are allowed by some states to treat foot pain and deteriorating bones from the knee down to the foot; other states limit them to the ankle and foot, and still others limit them to the foot only. It is common to see prescriptions written by these doctors for pain medication or drugs used to halt bone loss because these problems fall within the scope of authorized practice for a podiatrist to diagnose and treat. It would be a different situation altogether should a podiatrist write a prescription for a seizure medication. Obviously, the diagnosis and treatment of seizures would not be handled by a podiatrist; this is said to be beyond that practitioner's scope of authorized practice.

Ideally and technically, health care professionals should prescribe drugs related only to their line of work, but because prescribing medication is done in private and a diagnosis is not included on a prescription, it may be difficult or impossible for pharmacy personnel to determine whether prescribers are acting within their scope of authorized practice. Most of the time, it is fairly clear if a prescription is outside the prescriber's scope of practice, such as in the example of the podiatrist prescribing a seizure medication. Other times it is not, such as when a dentist prescribes a pain medication; pharmacy personnel do not know whether the pain medication is for a toothache within the dentist's scope or for a headache related to eye strain, which is not within a dentist's scope of practice. We can only assume the dentist is using it for something within his or her scope. Pharmacy personnel need to take extra steps to check on this only when it is clearly out of the prescriber's scope of practice or they have other reasons to doubt it.

To further complicate matters, many states have given prescribing rights to health care providers other than the traditional physicians, dentists, podiatrists, osteopaths, and veterinarians. In various states, these rights have been extended to chiropractors, registered nurse practitioners, physician's assistants, and pharmacists. The rules regarding prescribing rights vary from state to state. Some allow unrestricted prescribing for some categories of these "midlevel" prescribers and limit others to specific drugs, diseases, or situations. Many states require some midlevel practitioners to follow a protocol (or standard procedure and policy) that requires a physician's supervision over their prescribing, even to the point of requiring a physician to co-sign prescriptions for certain drugs; for example, a certified nurse practitioner may be able to write prescriptions for any medication, but physician's assistants may be required to have prescriptions co-signed by their supervising physicians. Pharmacists are often allowed to alter or adjust the dosing of medications for hospitalized patients. Each state's rules vary.

Questions regarding out-of-state prescribers also arise. The FDCA does not require the prescriber to be licensed in the state where the prescription is filled, provided the prescription is valid where it was written. However, the individual states have the right to determine whether prescriptions from out-of-state prescribers are valid.

Obviously, health care professionals are the only people who can prescribe medications, but some states allow certain people (e.g., a nurse or receptionist) to transmit the prescription or prescription refill to the pharmacy. Although they may transmit the information, they may not initiate or authorize a prescription or a refill. If this prescription information is sent by voice over the telephone, then the pharmacy employee must immediately "reduce the prescription or refill authorization to writing (that is, write down the information) and file it."

Approved versus Unapproved Uses

It is common practice for prescribers to prescribe a drug for a use or in a dosage not approved by the FDA or recommended by the labeling of the drug. These prescriptions may be filled without violating federal law. There are two reasons that it is legal to prescribe and dispense drugs for unapproved uses or in unapproved doses: new uses and doses for drugs are often discovered after FDA approval, and after articles about these new uses or doses are published in professional journals, it is acceptable medical practice to use this new information because it allows practice to keep up with the latest discoveries. The other reason is that the FDA is reluctant to interfere in the judgment of prescribers or the states' regulation of them.

In the past, manufacturers' sales representatives were prohibited from discussing unapproved uses for medications with prescribers, but the FDA Modernization Act of 1997 now allows them to provide this information, providing the information meets strict requirements.

DISPENSING REQUIREMENTS AND RESTRICTIONS

Labeling Requirements

Anyone who has ever seen prescription drug containers has realized that certain information must be included on the label before the medication can be dispensed.

By federal law, the label of the medication container must contain

- Name and address of dispenser (pharmacy)
- Serial number (Rx number)
- Date of prescription or filling (either one)
- Name of prescriber

If they are stated in the prescription, then the label must also include

- Name of patient
- Directions for use
- Cautionary statements (auxiliary labels)

You will notice how the first list is absolutely required and how the second is required only if stated in the prescription. Federal law leaves further requirements up to the states, so in addition to these federal requirements, individual states often have stricter label requirements that must be followed. Commonly, these are that the label must include the patient's name, the directions for use, and cautionary statements as well as the drug name, strength and quantity, and the pharmacist's initials. When taking a national examination such as the PTCB certification exam, you will want to remember which requirements apply to federal law and which may be from the individual state's laws and rules. The final contents of a prescription label are a combination of both state and federal rules.

If the medication is intended for animal or veterinary use and if a licensed veterinarian dispenses the drug, then the label must contain

- Name and address of the veterinarian
- Any directions for use and cautionary statements specified by the veterinarian

However, if the drug is dispensed by a pharmacy for animal use, then the label must contain

- Name and address of the pharmacy
- Serial number
- Date of the order or its filling
- Name of the veterinarian
- Directions for use and cautionary statements, if any, contained in such order

Again, state law may require more information on the label.

Patient Information and Cautionary Statements

Regarding labeling requirements, the FDCA assumes that the patient has received adequate instruction for use and precautions from the physician. As pharmacy professionals know, unfortunately this is not always the case. With the exception of certain drugs, federal regulations do not require prescription labels to contain directions for use or cautionary statements. However, several drugs must be dispensed by the pharmacy accompanied by an informational brochure, or patient package insert (PPI), that outlines many facts about the drug's use, side effects, precautions, and contraindications.

Such patient information brochures must be included with oral contraceptives, postcoital oral contraceptives (the so-called morning-after pill), diethylstilbestrol, injectable contraceptives, medroxyprogesterone acetate, estrogens, and progestational (fertility drug) prescriptions.

The drug manufacturer supplies these package inserts, usually by including several of them with each bottle the pharmacy buys from the wholesaler. It is the pharmacy's responsibility to provide the PPIs to the patient. This must be done when one of four things occurs:

1. When a prescription for a listed medication is first filled
2. Any time at the patient's request
3. Before the first dose given in a hospital
4. Every 30 days in a hospital

This does not reduce the pharmacist's responsibility to counsel the patient on each prescription; patient consultation remains one of the main functions of a pharmacist. Well-informed patients are much more likely to follow their doctor's orders regarding drug use, which is bound to result in better health and more efficient use of drugs and the money that is spent on them. Supplying written information is an effective way of supplementing a pharmacist's consultation, but in no way replaces or diminishes the importance and impact of personal consultation.

Compounding versus Manufacturing

As a routine part of the dispensing process, pharmacies often compound, or make up, products as specifically ordered by a prescriber (topical creams and ointments are perhaps the most common of these) when there is no commercial product that fits the patient's needs. This routine prescription compounding is sometimes questioned: when is a pharmacy simply filling legitimate prescription requests, and when is it manufacturing (an activity that requires a different license and Drug Enforcement Administration [DEA] number)? To clarify this question, the FDA issued compounding guidelines to help both pharmacies and law enforcement officials in determining when a pharmacy has crossed the line into manufacturing. Any of the following activities are considered to be those of a manufacturer, and a pharmacy doing any of these could be prosecuted for doing something it was not licensed to do:

- Soliciting business to compound products
- Compounding regularly or in excessively large amounts products that are commercially available and are essentially generic copies of commercially available products
- Using commercial-scale equipment
- Compounding excessively large amounts of a product in anticipation of receiving valid prescriptions
- Offering compounded products at wholesale prices with the intent for them to be resold at retail prices
- Distributing excessively large amounts of compounded products

A few other conditions also apply, but these are the main concerns for a pharmacy. Note that compounding a product to fill a prescription is perfectly legal, as is making a "batch" of something to more easily fill prescriptions that are expected to be received in the near future. The six situations listed are beyond the scope of filling prescriptions or preparing for expected prescriptions.

The Orange Book

To provide guidance to pharmacists in choosing which generic products are appropriate to use for generic substitution, the FDA produces a book called *Approved Drug Products with Therapeutic Equivalence Evaluations*, commonly referred to as the Orange Book because of its distinctive orange cover. This book rates products for therapeutic equivalence, which really means biologic equivalence (or bioequivalence) in that they have comparable absorption characteristics. An example of this would be if several manufacturers each market their own products of atenolol, a medication affecting blood pressure and heart rate. The Orange Book would outline which ones were comparable and could safely be used interchangeably.

The Orange Book uses a two-letter code to rate bioequivalence. Products beginning with the letter "A" are considered therapeutically equivalent; those beginning with "B" are not. Pharmacists should limit their generic substitution choices to those products with an "A" rating, because of the appropriateness for patient care and state laws. Following the Orange Book is not a federal requirement, but it is a guide to help in following state laws and many insurance company regulations that require bioequivalence or therapeutic equivalence for generic substitution.

Inspections

State pharmacy boards have inspectors that routinely look over the records and inventories of pharmacies. They typically not only visit each registered pharmacy on a regular basis, but also will conduct additional inspections if a problem is reported or suspected. Also, the FDA and DEA may inspect a pharmacy, but their inspections are usually in response to a complaint or suspected illegal activity. Some of these inspections require them to have a legal search warrant; others (typically the routine state inspector's visits) do not. DEA agents are required to provide the pharmacy with a Form 82, "Notice of Inspection." In any case, they should immediately be referred to the pharmacist in charge, and all personnel should cooperate with their requests. As a word of caution, pharmacy technicians should respond fully to their requests and questions but not volunteer more than requested. The inspectors want specific answers to specific questions, and adding more information can confuse the situation and lead to more issues that might not have needed to be addressed.

Packaging

To package a drug, the container must meet standards established by certain national professional groups. Also, with the passing of the Poison Prevention Packaging Act (PPPA) of 1970, all prescriptions for solid oral dosage forms (that is, tablets and capsules for oral use) and for all controlled substances must meet "special packaging" requirements. That is, the container must be designed or constructed to be difficult for children 5 years of age and younger to open. These containers are then referred to as *child-resistant containers*.

All prescriptions for solid oral dosage forms must be dispensed in child-resistant containers, with the following exceptions:

- Sublingual doses of nitroglycerin
- Sublingual and chewable forms or isosorbide dinitrate in dosing forms containing 10 mg or less
- Erythromycin ethylsuccinate granules for oral suspension and oral suspension in packages containing not more than 8 g of erythromycin
- Anhydrous cholestyramine in powder form
- All unit doses of potassium supplements
- Sodium fluoride drug preparations containing less than 264 mg of sodium fluoride per package
- Betamethasone tablets containing in the package less than 12.6 mg of the drug
- Pancrelipase preparations
- Prednisone in tablet form when dispensed in packages containing not more than 105 mg of the drug
- Mebendazole in tablet form in packages containing not more than 600 mg of the drug
- Methylprednisolone in tablet form in packages containing not more than 84 mg of the drug
- Colestipol in powder form in packages containing not more than 5 g of the drug
- Erythromycin ethylsuccinate in tablet form in packages containing no more than 16 g of erythromycin

Drugs exempt from the PPPA include

- Drugs dispensed to patients in hospitals.
- Prescription drugs distributed by manufacturers in bulk "stock bottles" without special packaging provided that they intend the pharmacist to repackage the drug prior to dispensing. However, when the manufacturer distributes a prescription drug to pharmacies in containers designed to be dispensed to the consumer in that container with only the addition of a label, then the manufacturer's container must conform to the special packaging requirements.

What happens when someone requests a non-child-resistant or easy-open container? If the prescriber or the patient requests an easy open container, then the pharmacist may dispense the prescription using a non-childproof container. The law does specify that patients may request that all of their prescriptions be dispensed in non-child-resistant containers, but a prescriber may only request this for individual prescriptions. This distinction, which the courts have not ruled on, is not routinely given much attention.

Pharmacies should require the patient to sign a written request to use non-childproof containers. The PPPA law allows a patient to make this request verbally, but written and signed statements hold up much better in court, and most pharmacies now keep a log book or use standard forms for the patient to sign.

In addition to prescription drugs, OTC aspirin and 18 other specified OTC drugs must be in child-resistant containers. Manufacturers are allowed one exception: they may have one single size of package in a non-child-resistant container as long as there are other sizes that are child resistant. For example, as long as there are some packages of aspirin that are child resistant, a manufacturer or distributor may also sell one package size that is not; this is to accommodate those adults who have trouble opening child-resistant containers, such as the very elderly or infirm or those with arthritis or other problems that make opening these containers difficult. By marketing both types of containers, young children can be protected when their parents choose a product in a child-resistant container, and adults who are unable to open child-resistant containers can handle their own medication bottles. To reduce possible confusion and mistakes, the warning "This package for households without young children" or "Package not child resistant" must be printed on the package in bold capital letters.

It is interesting to note that this legislation also forbids the reuse of any part of a prescription container that is made of plastic. Child-resistant containers function using the flexibility of plastic; when the plastic is bent or compressed from pressure, the cap and vial connect through interlocking molded parts. After a period of use, the plastic weakens (through repetitive opening and closing with dose after dose), and the container loses its child-resistant feature. Therefore, when refilling a prescription, the pharmacy may not reuse any plastic part of a child-resistant container.

Mailing

If a patient wishes to have a prescription sent by mail, then a few regulations must be followed by the pharmacy sending the medication.

Most drugs may legally be mailed. When a prescription is mailed, an inner container (e.g., the prescription vial) must be properly labeled and securely sealed with a child-resistant cap. A plain outer container or wrapper must cover the inner container so there is no indication of the contents. Poisons, alcohol, and flammables may not be mailed.

Note that these are U.S. Postal Service regulations, and that delivery services not associated with the U.S. Postal Service need not follow these regulations.

The Robinson-Patman Act

The Robinson-Patman Act is of special interest in that it makes it illegal for sellers to charge different prices for the same product when the price difference could hurt competition. This arises if, for example, a wholesaler charges two different pharmacies two different prices for the same product. If these two pharmacies were competing with each other (perhaps they were located in the same part of town), then this price difference would be illegal.

There are, however, two exceptions to this law. First, if the pharmacies are not competing with each other, which could be because they are located far enough apart not to compete for customers (e.g., two drugstores on opposite sides of a large city) or because they do not compete at all, such as if one were a retail drugstore and the other were a hospital using the product for its own use. A hospital's own use means providing drugs for (1) inpatients, (2) emergency room patients, (3) patients to be discharged, (4) employees, and (5) patients receiving treatment with the drug product on the hospital premises. A hospital that also runs an outpatient pharmacy for the general public must buy the drugs used in that retail pharmacy from the same sources at the same prices as other retail pharmacies; a retail outlet operated by a hospital may not sell products purchased by the hospital at a special discount. It must buy its own inventory at the same prices as competing retail pharmacies. The other exception is whether a pharmacy qualifies for large-volume discounts. Price differences are legal if one of the outlets is so much bigger that it can place an order large enough to qualify for a volume discount, even if it is located close enough to another to be competitive and is operating a similar business.

RECALLS

Unfortunately, sometimes after a drug has been approved and is in widespread use, adverse effects and events become more significant than the NDA studies suggested. If these events are severe enough, then the

FDA may suggest that the drug manufacturer recall a product or even order it to do so. Recalls are classified according to severity:

- A Class I recall is for when a product will cause serious or fatal consequences.
- A Class II recall is for when a product may cause serious but reversible adverse effects.
- A Class III recall is for a problem that is not likely to cause adverse health consequences.

This classification is also used when a manufacturing or distribution problem causes a drug to be adulterated, such as when a product was stored or shipped improperly or when there is a problem with the manufacturing process.

Depending on how widely distributed and how potentially harmful the problem is, many methods can be used to notify the public of the recall. Television notifications, printed warnings and personal telephone calls can all be used, but the most common is a letter or telegram to pharmacies, hospitals, and prescribers. The general public is rarely informed of a drug recall, mostly because there are few Class I or Class II recalls. Almost all are Class III recalls caused by contamination, improper contents, wrong amounts, or storage and distribution problems such as poor temperature control or dirty storage conditions. Class I and II problems are usually related to the drug's pharmacological actions, which are normally noticed during preapproval IND studies.

SAMPLE QUESTIONS FOR STUDENT REVIEW

1. What is adulteration?
2. How does the cleanliness of the factory, storage facility, or transportation system affect adulteration of a drug product?
3. Give two examples of misbranding.
4. What is the seven-point label required for OTC drugs?
5. What other things must be on an OTC product label?
6. How can a physician or other prescriber obtain drug samples?
7. List the four points that characterize a drug.
8. List the factors that characterize a new drug. What is the exception to this?
9. Describe the three phases of an IND application.
10. Which prescribers may write prescriptions or hospital orders for investigational drugs?

11. Why did the Drug Price Competition and Patent-Term Restoration Act of 1984 come about? What does it do for generic drug manufacturers? What does it do for innovator or pioneer drug manufacturers?
12. What type of drugs does the Orphan Drug Act help bring to market?
13. Which determines who may prescribe medications, the state governments or the federal government?
14. What is meant by a scope of practice?
15. May a prescriber order a drug for a use or dose that is not approved by the FDA?
16. Which determines most of what must be on a prescription label, the state governments or the federal government?
17. What items does the FDCA require be placed on a prescription label?
18. When is it required to provide a patient with a package insert?
19. What is within the scope of the term *compounding*, and when do a pharmacy's activities become manufacturing?
20. What is the Orange Book?
21. May patients request that their prescriptions not be dispensed in child-resistant containers?
22. What type of dosing forms must be in child-resistant containers?
23. When and why is there often one size of an OTC product that is not in a child-resistant container?
24. Which parts of a child-resistant prescription vial may not be reused?
25. To send a prescription via the U.S. Postal Service, what must not be on the outer wrapping?
26. List and define the different classes of drug recalls.

4

FEDERAL CONTROLLED SUBSTANCE ACT OF 1970

OVERVIEW AND OBJECTIVES

Humankind has utilized dangerous and addictive medicines since prehistoric times, but with the increasing urbanization of the population and the changes in social structure that brings about, as well as the modern ability to synthesize new forms of drugs, the problems created by dangerous and addictive drugs were too much to be dealt with by families and communities alone. The government had made fitful, stuttering efforts at piecemeal controls dealing with narrow topics but had not addressed the major problems until the landmark Controlled Substance Act (CSA) in 1970. This act replaced more than 50 other minor pieces of legislation with a new concept and approach to regulation: limit and register those who are to be legally allowed to handle such substances. Anyone not registered is acting illegally, and those who are registered have narrowly defined rules of behavior to follow.

This act provides methods to control drugs that are considered dangerous through their potential for addiction and abuse. To regulate these controlled substances, the CSA created a closed system of manufacture, distribution, prescription, and dispensing by registering each entity in the system with a registration number provided by the responsible federal agency, the Drug Enforcement Administration (DEA).

Only businesses, institutions, and people registered by the DEA may legally handle controlled substances, which thereby provides a method of managing these products and keeping them out of illegal channels.

Chapter 4 discusses the following subjects:

■ Registration requirements and procedures
■ Handling and storage of controlled substances
■ Record keeping
■ Prescribing requirements
■ Dispensing requirements

CONTROL SCHEDULES

Definitions

When the CSA was enacted into law, controlled substances were divided into five categories or schedules. The attorney general has the authority to decide in which schedule a drug will be placed, and placement among the schedules is based on the controlled substance's potential for abuse. Schedule I drugs have the highest potential for abuse; Schedule V controlled substances have a relatively low potential for abuse. A pharmacy usually dispenses controlled substances from a manufacturer's stock bottle, and this bottle, by law, must be labeled with a capital letter "C" and the Roman numeral from whichever schedule the controlled substance is listed. A hyphen may also separate the two. For example, CII, CIII, CIV, and CV may be printed on the stock bottle, or the label could be printed with C-II, C-III, C-IV, and C-V.

Schedules

Of all drugs, C-I substances have the highest potential for abuse. These drugs have no currently accepted medical use in the United States and lack proof of safety for use under medical supervision. Included in Schedule I are numerous opiate derivatives such as heroin, as well as hallucinogens such as marijuana and LSD. By law, these drugs may not be prescribed and are only legally seen in some research situations.

C-II substances have a high potential for abuse. Abuse of such drugs may lead to severe psychological or physical dependence on those substances. Schedule II controlled substances are currently accepted for medical use in the United States. Included in this schedule are opium powder and its derivatives morphine, cocaine, and codeine. Stimulants commonly used to treat attention disorders, including methylphenidate and amphetamine, are also included in Schedule II.

C-III controlled substances have a lower potential for abuse than those drugs in Schedule II. These drugs have a currently accepted medical use in treatment in the United States. Abuse of these substances may lead to low-to-moderate physical dependence or high psychological dependence.

C-IV controlled substances have a lower potential for abuse than any controlled substances in Schedules I through III. These substances have a currently accepted use in treatment in the United States. Abuse of such substances may lead to limited physical or psychological dependence.

C-V controlled substances have a lower potential for abuse than any of the drugs in the other schedules. The drugs in Schedule V have a currently accepted medical use in treatment in the United States. Abuse of these substances may lead to less-limited physical or psychological dependence than that of the controlled substances in Schedules I through IV. Usually, substances in Schedule V contain codeine plus other active ingredients.

Schedule	Accepted Use	Abuse Potential	Dependence Level
C-I	None	High	Lack of accepted safety
C-II	Accepted	High	Severe psychological or physical
C-III	Accepted	Less	Moderate-to-low physical or high physical
C-IV	Accepted	Less	Limited physical or psychological
C-V	Accepted	Less	Limited physical or psychological

Some narcotic drugs are listed both in Schedule II and in lower schedules, thereby causing some confusion. The most common of these is codeine, which by itself (e.g., codeine sulfate 30-mg tablets) is a C-II item but, when mixed with other ingredients (such as in Tylenol no. 3 tablets, a combination of 325 mg acetaminophen and 30 mg codeine) is C-III. The key here is the addition of other active ingredients, which allows a substance such as codeine to be in more than one schedule even when the amount of codeine per tablet is the same. Concentration per dose also can influence the schedule assignment, such as for Robitussin AC, a C-V item because of its low amount of codeine per dose. In this manner, codeine and combination products containing codeine are listed in three different controlled substance schedules.

In addition, a law passed in March 2006 created a new category called Scheduled Listed Chemical Products to control the over-the-counter (OTC) sales of pseudoephedrine, ephedrine, and phenylpropanolamine to combat the illegal manufacture of methamphetamine. The requirements of this new category will be examined fully in this chapter in the discussion of dispensing requirements and restrictions.

REGISTRATION

Who Must Register

The DEA does not determine who can be licensed to conduct certain activities. This is determined by the individual states; those the state allows to handle or prescribe controlled substances must register with the DEA.

The federal CSA regulates practitioners handling controlled substances and the activities these practitioners conduct. Numerous activities require registration with the DEA. Anyone who manufactures or distributes controlled substances must annually obtain registration to carry out these activities. Any person or pharmacy that dispenses controlled substances must obtain registration. After approval, these registrations last at least 1 year but no more than 3 years.

Each of the following activities requires registration:

- Manufacturing controlled substances.
- Distributing controlled substances.
- Dispensing controlled substances.
- Conducting research with controlled substances classed in Schedules II through V. In exception to this rule, if the registrant is also registered to conduct some other activity, then this person does not need additional separate registration to conduct research.
- Conducting instructional activities with controlled substances in Schedules II through V.
- Conducting a narcotic treatment program using narcotic drugs from Schedules II through V. In exception to this rule, if treatment is conducted at more than one treatment location, then each site must hold its own separate registration.
- Conducting research and instructional activities with Schedule I controlled substances.
- Conducting chemical analysis with controlled substances from any schedule.
- Importing controlled substances.
- Exporting controlled substances.
- Acting as a compounder for a treatment program, as someone who mixes, prepares, packages, or changes the dosage form of narcotic controlled substances in Schedules II through V for use by a narcotic addiction treatment program.

What a Registrant May Do

Generally, practitioners must be registered separately for every activity in which they are involved. An exception to this rule allows activities that are closely associated with the registered activity as long as these closely associated activities take place at the same location as the registered activity. These are called *coincident activities*, and separate registration is not required. Coincident activities are discussed in relation to each mandatory registered activity.

When registrants are manufacturers, they are involved in an activity that includes the production, preparation, compounding, or processing of a drug or substance by extraction or synthesis. Packaging, repackaging, labeling, and relabeling also fall into the manufacturing category. A business that is registered to manufacture may also distribute that same substance without holding separate registration as a distributor under the coincident activities clause. Another recognized coincident activity involves conducting chemical analysis and preclinical research. These activities may be conducted by a manufacturer without additional registration.

An exemption to the manufacturing registration requirement refers to pharmacies that compound prescriptions. A pharmacy is exempt from the manufacturing registration if the substance is compounded for routine prescription dispensing and is an aqueous, oleaginous solution or dosage form composed of 20% or less of a narcotic controlled substance. Compounding any prescription that contains a higher percentage of a narcotic controlled substance requires separate registration as a manufacturer.

To *distribute* means to deliver. Dispensing and administering are not in the same category as distribution. Registered distributors are usually drug wholesalers. Although no coincident activities are allowed for distributors, a pharmacy may sometimes be recognized as a limited distributor. When pharmacies distribute controlled substances to other registrants, such as different pharmacies or physicians, this is known as *limited distribution* and is allowed as a coincident activity under their dispenser's registration. This coincident activity practice may occur only if the amount of controlled substances distributed does not exceed 5% of the total amount of controlled substances distributed and dispensed by the pharmacy. If a pharmacy does exceed the 5% limit, then it must register as a distributor.

A *practitioner* is one who dispenses. Hospitals, pharmacies, and professionals who can prescribe controlled substances are all considered practitioners. Pharmacists and nurses do not have their own separate registration numbers, but individual practitioners such as physicians, physicians' assistants, nurse practitioners, dentists, and investigators do. For pharmacists and nurses, their place of employment — a pharmacy or a hospital — is the registrant.

Narcotic treatment programs are divided into two categories: maintenance or detoxification programs. *Maintenance programs* use narcotic controlled substances to treat those who are dependent on heroin or other opiate drugs. Decreasing doses of specific narcotic controlled substances are given to these patients to "step down" their addiction. By using these decreasing doses, patients are basically weaned off their addiction into, it is hoped, a drug-free state. *Detoxification programs* also use narcotic controlled substances to wean people off dangerous drugs, but in a more acute situation. Every individual practitioner or dispenser involved in a narcotic treatment program must be separately registered. If this practitioner handles controlled substances outside the narcotic treatment program, then separate registration must also be obtained for this activity. Therefore, to be a "compounder" for a narcotic treatment program, a pharmacy must be registered separately for this activity. As described, a *compounder* is a pharmacy that mixes, prepares, packages, or changes the dosage form of controlled substances in Schedules II through V for use in a narcotic treatment program. A pharmacy, hospital, or individual practitioner may then end up with two DEA numbers: one for its regular practice and another for the narcotic treatment program. No coincident activities are recognized in this category.

If a narcotic treatment program treats patients at more than one site and narcotic controlled substances are kept at these multiple sites, then each site must be separately registered with the DEA.

In addition to the activities requiring registration and the associated coincident activities listed, many exemptions to these rules exist. For example, employees and agents of registrants are exempt from registration. Pharmacists, pharmacy technicians, pharmacy interns, and nurses are not required to register personally with the DEA as long as their employers — hospitals or pharmacies — are registered. In addition, those who have part ownership in a hospital or pharmacy but are not practitioners, pharmacists, pharmacy workers, or direct participants in daily operations are not required to hold separate registration with the DEA.

As stated, employees of a registered hospital do not require separate registration. Also, practitioners employed by a hospital who practice only for that hospital do not require separate registration. However, if a practitioner writes a prescription for a controlled substance that will be filled by a pharmacy outside the hospital, that practitioner must be individually registered. In addition, the hospital pharmacy may not fill a controlled substance prescription from a nonindividually registered practitioner if the hospital pharmacy itself is registered as a practitioner separately from the hospital.

Practitioners in settings within the Veterans' Administration (VA) have fewer restrictions. If they follow certain rules, then unregistered employees — interns, residents, foreign-trained physicians, and VA physicians — may dispense, administer, and prescribe controlled substances within the VA system. State law must first allow these people to do so. Also, prescribing must be done within the usual course of employment in the hospital. Finally, these individuals must be authorized by the hospital to do so. A specific internal code is assigned to each prescriber; the code is attached as a suffix, separated by a hyphen, to the institution's DEA number. If any of these VA prescribers practice in a private setting, then separate registration must be obtained from the DEA.

Public Health Service prescribers, Bureau of Prison prescribers, and military prescribers may prescribe, administer, and dispense in the usual course of their official duties without separate registration. Controlled substance prescriptions must contain the prescriber's branch of service and service number. If any of these prescribers practices in a private setting, then separate registration must be obtained from the DEA.

Although law enforcement laboratories must register with the DEA, law enforcement personnel and civil defense officials do not need to register to handle controlled substances.

Security and Storage

In addition to comprehensive laws regarding record keeping, which are discussed in a separate section, maintaining security over controlled substances and properly storing them are very important issues.

Two ways to store controlled substances are recognized by the DEA. By following either of these methods, the theft of controlled substances ideally will be minimized. Controlled substances can either be kept together in a securely constructed, locked cabinet or dispersed throughout the pharmacy. Many pharmacies lock up only Schedule II controlled substances and then alphabetically disperse the remaining controlled substances throughout the rest of their stock. Other pharmacies disperse all of the controlled substances throughout their stock just like all other products.

OBTAINING CONTROLLED SUBSTANCES

Who May Place Orders

The procedure for ordering and obtaining controlled substances is different from ordering and receiving noncontrolled drugs.

To obtain Schedule II substances, a DEA Form 222 or triplicate order form must be used (see Appendix 5). The DEA issues these order forms to be distributed to registrants on request. The forms contain the registrant's name, address, DEA number, and the schedules the registrant is allowed to order. Each order form is individually numbered.

The people who signed the applications for registration with the DEA are the people who must sign the completed 222 order forms. If these people are unable to sign the 222 order form, then they may delegate that authority to someone else by filing a letter of power of attorney. This is a statement that gives another person the authority to act on their behalf; in this case, it gives someone the power to sign 222 forms on behalf of the originally authorized people.

The DEA 222 form must be perfectly filled out — erasures, cross-outs, typeovers, or any kind of editing are not allowed. If a mistake or typing error is made, then the form must be voided and filed away and another form used.

When the order is placed, the buyer keeps Copy 3 of the 222 form and sends the first two copies to the supplier, who then forwards Copy 2 to the DEA. In this way, the DEA has records of all legal C-II purchases. When the purchaser receives the order from the supplier, the recipient completes Copy 3, which has extra spaces on the right in which to record the actual number of packages received as well as the date and the checking person's initials.

The DEA now allows a purchaser to complete the 222 order form online through the supplying wholesaler. There are forms available to download from and return to the DEA, followed by some requirements for the wholesaler to complete to be registered for online ordering of C-II items. The advantage of online ordering is usually faster delivery, but more importantly the pharmacy now has all 222 records available electronically and does not have to store them in paper form. In addition, no one has to use the archaic triplicate 222 form with carbon paper between the copies.

On a day-to-day basis, numerous C-II prescriptions may leave a pharmacy. Sometimes, a pharmacy may not have enough of a C-II substance to complete an order and may have to obtain the drug from another pharmacy to fill the prescription. When a registrant pharmacy wishes to obtain Schedule II controlled substances from another pharmacy, the pharmacist ordering the C-II controlled substance must complete a DEA Form 222 just as if it were being purchased from a wholesaler. The ordering pharmacy retains Copy 3, and the supplying pharmacy receives the first two copies and forwards Copy 2 to the DEA. The complete 222 form procedure must take place, even if the two pharmacies are only lending and borrowing the drug without exchanging money.

Occasionally, a physician may wish to have some C-II items on hand for office use. This also requires a DEA 222 form before the physician can obtain the product, with the same requirements as listed for pharmacies. A physician may not use a standard prescription blank to order C-II items for office use; the complete 222 form procedure is required.

Ordering controlled substances in Schedules III through V does not require as much work as ordering and obtaining controlled substances in

Schedule II. The DEA allows the purchaser to use routine purchase order forms or invoices just like any other purchase. Again, a physician who wants some C-III, C-IV, or C-V products on hand for office use may not use a standard prescription blank to order them. The physician's office must issue an invoice or purchase order the same as if buying anything else from another vendor.

RECORD KEEPING

Records Kept by a Pharmacy

Maintaining an accurate record of all prescriptions is important for a pharmacy, and the law allows the filing of prescriptions in any one of three approved ways:

1. Three separate prescription files may be kept — one file for C-II controlled substances, one for C-III through C-V controlled substances, and one for all other prescriptions.
2. A pharmacy may choose to keep two individual files. In this two-file system, one file contains only C-II controlled substance prescriptions, and the second file contains all other prescriptions. Because the second file has prescriptions from both scheduled and nonscheduled prescriptions (Rxs), the DEA requires that the scheduled Rxs be marked in a way that will make them easier to identify. The requirement is that all C-III through C-V controlled substance prescriptions must be stamped with a 1-inch high red C in the lower right-hand corner.
3. Another two-file system may be kept. In this system, all controlled substance prescriptions are kept in one file, where again the C-III through C-V controlled substances are identified by the 1-inch red C. The second file contains all nonscheduled Rxs. Note that in all of these choices of filing, the C-II Rxs never need the red C stamp.

Interestingly, if the pharmacy's computer system allows a technician to find prescription information by prescription number, prescriber's name, patient's name, drug, and date, the red C stamp may be omitted.

Maintaining inventory records is another important topic. According to the federal CSA, a beginning inventory of all controlled substances on hand — controlled substances ordered and inventoried by the pharmacy — is required on the date the pharmacy first dispenses controlled substances. Every 24 months or sooner after this initial inventory, a new inventory of controlled substances must be conducted. The pharmacy may choose how often to do these updated inventories, but it must be no longer than 24 months since the last one.

When controlled substances are inventoried, an exact count must be taken for C-I and C-II controlled substances. The quantity of C-III, C-IV, and C-V controlled substances may be estimated unless the container holds more than 1000 dosage units. In this case, an exact count is necessary.

Pharmacies must also maintain accurate records of acquisition. Executed and completed federal order forms for C-I and C-II controlled substances (DEA Form 222) must be kept. Routine packaging lists and invoices are sufficient for maintaining records of C-III through C-V controlled substances. These records must be readily retrievable, so they must be kept on the premises of the pharmacy for at least 2 years. Individual states may require a longer time period. An exception to this allows chain stores or hospitals to keep certain financial and shipping records (but not 222 forms, prescriptions, or inventory records) at a central location if they first notify the DEA of their intention to do so. Of course, if the pharmacy uses online electronic ordering of C-II items, the record-keeping details for C-II purchases are reduced to filing the packaging lists and invoices, just as for C-III through C-V purchases, as long as the C-II records are kept in a separate file.

Each state can decide to allow certain C-V products to be sold over the counter without a prescription, providing that proper records of the sale are kept. These are antidiarrheal items and cough preparations, and the pharmacy must keep a log book to record each sale. Because there is no physician or other prescriber involved in such a sale, only a registered pharmacist is allowed to handle this interaction, although once the registered pharmacist has determined the validity of the request, the actual sale and delivery can be handled by another staff person. The limit regarding how much one person can purchase is no more than 240 ml or 48 solid dosage forms of anything containing opium, and no more than half that much (120 ml or 24 solid dosage units) of any other C-V item in any given 48-hour period. Also, the purchaser must be at least 18 years of age and show proper identification. Therefore, the log book for these OTC C-V sales must include the following information to keep track of this:

Purchaser's name and address
Name and quantity of the product purchased
Date of each sale
Initials of registered pharmacist

This log book must be kept for 2 years, just like other federal record-keeping requirements. Remember, your state may specify a different time span for keeping records.

Records Kept by an Institution

An *institution* is a hospital, nursing home, clinic, or extended-care facility. Its records of purchases, other acquisitions, and inventory levels must be kept in the same manner as those for a pharmacy.

Institutions differ from pharmacies in that they must also record the number of units dispensed to each individual patient, the name and address of the person receiving the substance, written or typewritten name or initials of the individual who dispensed or administered the substance, and any other kind of dispersal information that may be appropriate, such as the patient's room number, time of day, and the remaining balance of the controlled substance on hand. This is usually done by a medication administration record sheet kept in each patient care area. The nurse or other caregiver fills out this administration record sheet each time a dose is given to a patient.

Records Kept by an Individual Practitioner

An *individual practitioner* is a person who is licensed to prescribe controlled substances. Two sets of rules for practitioners exist, and depending on the category in to which prescribers fall, they will follow the set of rules established for them. Two factors determine which regulations are followed: the activity of the practitioner and whether the practitioner charges patients for controlled substances.

If the practitioner writes prescriptions for controlled substances (such as a physician during an office visit) or administers controlled substances without charging for them separately from the treatment fee (perhaps during a treatment in the doctor's office), then the practitioner is exempt from record keeping other than the routine office visit notes and records. However, if the practitioner regularly dispenses or administers to the patient controlled substances for later self-administration and charges the patient for these substances separately from the office visit or treatment charge, then the practitioner must maintain the same records as an institution.

Records Maintained by a Narcotic Treatment Program

Narcotic treatment programs adhere to the same rules as institutions, with a few notable additions. Narcotic treatment programs must maintain a dispensing log at the site of the dispensing. This log contains the name and strength of each narcotic substance dispensed, the dosage form, the date dispensed, the identification of the patient, the amount administered or furnished to the patient to take home, and the dispenser's initials.

PRESCRIBING REQUIREMENTS AND RESTRICTIONS

Who May Prescribe (see also Appendix 8)

Practitioners are not licensed by the federal government. The state regulates who is allowed to prescribe medication, including controlled substances. Traditional prescribers are considered to be physicians, osteopaths, dentists, and veterinarians. In some instances, podiatrists are also included as traditional prescribers. Practitioners must be licensed in the state where they practice and must also be registered with the DEA or be exempt from registration. These traditional prescribers may prescribe any legal medication.

Today, many states also recognize what many classify as nontraditional prescribers, often called midlevel practitioners. Midlevel practitioners may include physician's assistants, certified nurse practitioners, and pharmacists. In certain states, these individuals may prescribe medication; however, unfortunately state law is not consistent. In some states, nontraditional prescribers may prescribe all drugs except controlled substances; other states may allow these practitioners limited controlled substance prescribing rights. It is important to note that any individual who prescribes controlled substances must be registered with the DEA.

DEA Numbers for Prescribers

After individuals have registered with the DEA, they are assigned unique DEA identification numbers. DEA numbers consist of nine characters. The first two characters are letters. The first letter is either A, B, M, or P. An A or B signifies a prescriber with full prescriptive rights. The M signifies a midlevel prescriber with limited prescriptive rights, and a P signifies a distributor. The second letter is the first letter of the registrant's last name. The third through eighth characters are unique to the individual registrant. The ninth and last digit is known as the verification number. To verify that a DEA number is indeed valid, a simple formula can be used: add the first, third, and fifth digits. To that number, add twice the sum of the second, fourth, and sixth digits. The rightmost digit of this sum should correspond to the ninth digit in the registrant's DEA number.

Let us look at an example of a valid DEA number. If Jane Smith, M.D., uses the number BS2473293, is it a valid number? The B is appropriate for a physician, the S is the first letter of her last name, and the numbers can be checked by following the guides outlined: add the first, third, and fifth digits $(2 + 7 + 2 = 11)$; add the second, fourth, and sixth digits and double the answer $(4 + 3 + 9 = 16 \times 2 = 32)$. Then, add the two sums $(11 + 32 = 43)$. The last digit of this sum should match the ninth digit of the DEA number for it to be a valid number. This validation check can be used whenever there is doubt regarding the legality or validity of a prescription or prescriber. Of course, an informed criminal could fabricate a number that fits this, but it is unlikely.

Purpose of Prescription

Obviously, prescriptions are written by prescribers to treat a specific medical condition. These practitioners may issue a prescription only for a legitimate medical purpose that falls within their scope of practice. If a practitioner is simply furnishing prescriptions to patients with no real reason (e.g., to sustain a narcotic abuser), then this is considered illegitimate practice.

The *usual scope of practice* refers to practitioners acting in the usual course of their profession. For example, if a podiatrist were to prescribe a medication for a toothache, then this certainly does not fall within the normal scope of practice of treating medical problems of the foot.

Both the prescriber and pharmacist share joint responsibility for the legitimacy of the treatment of a medical condition. Unfortunately, in the usual course of business, a pharmacist has no way of knowing which diagnosis a practitioner has made. This is not a problem as long as the available information gives the pharmacist no reason to suspect wrongdoing. If a reasonable and prudent person would have no reason to be suspicious, then the law relieves the pharmacist of liability for an illegal prescription. However, when a pharmacist actually knows that a prescriber has issued a prescription for a condition outside the normal scope of practice, the pharmacist may not legally dispense the medication. To help deal with this problem, the DEA has published a list of conditions to which pharmacists can refer if they suspect abuse of drugs or an abuse of privileges:

- Does the prescriber write prescriptions for significantly larger amounts of controlled substances than other prescribers in the area?
- Is the dose, quantity, or combination of prescribed drugs outside accepted medical usage?
- Are irrational combinations prescribed frequently and concurrently?
- Are patients presenting prescriptions for drugs of abuse coming from outside your normal patient community? Do they arrive in groups with prescriptions from the same prescriber?

■ Do patients appear to be returning too frequently?

By taking these guidelines into consideration, a pharmacy staff member may be better able to make a sound decision regarding the legitimacy of the prescription in question. Although many states are requiring tamper-resistant prescription forms for controlled substances utilizing "safety" paper with watermarks, colored threads, or special surface coating such as we now see on personal checks and paper money, these old tried-and-true methods for spotting forged or altered prescriptions are still good pharmacy practice.

Addiction Treatment Restrictions

According to the CSA, an individual prescriber may not issue a prescription for a narcotic drug for the purpose of detoxifying or maintenance treatment of an addicted patient. The reasoning behind this law is simple: narcotic treatment programs and the prescribers who work with them must adhere to stricter reporting and security measures and must be separately registered with the DEA for their work within a detoxification or narcotic addiction treatment program.

An exception can be made in the case of emergency treatment of withdrawal symptoms, when an individual practitioner may admit the patient to the hospital and administer narcotic drugs to help relieve withdrawal symptoms for a maximum period of 3 days. During this time, the practitioner must arrange for the admission of the patient to a proper detox or treatment program. Also, if treatment program patients are admitted to a hospital for treatment of another medical condition or injuries from an accident, they may be treated for their narcotic addiction while in the hospital for the other reason.

Requirements for the Prescription Form

In addition to the standard requirements outlined by the Food, Drug, and Cosmetic Act (FDCA), a written prescription for any controlled substance must also

■ Contain the full name and address of the patient
■ Contain the name, address, and DEA number of the prescriber
■ Be written in ink, indelible pencil, or typewritten
■ Bear the date it was issued (pre-dating or postdating is not allowed)
■ Be manually signed by the practitioner on the date of issue (signature stamps are not allowed)

Individual state pharmacy boards may require that some additional topics be included on a prescription.

Fax Requirements and Restrictions (see also Appendix 7)

Any prescription may be faxed, but C-II controlled substances may not be filled until the pharmacy is presented with the original handwritten prescription. An exception to this is that nursing home orders, home infusion orders, and hospice orders may all be faxed and dispensed regardless of their schedule. In these cases, the faxed copy is considered to be the original hardcopy.

Regulations vary quite a bit from state to state, so it is important to recognize the unique rules for the state where a pharmacy professional practices.

Prescribing C-II Products

The original handwritten prescription must be presented to the pharmacy when requesting a C-II controlled substance. The only exception to this rule is in the event of an emergency, when an oral prescription may be accepted, providing it meets certain criteria.

In the case of an emergency, it can be assumed that the prescriber has determined that treatment with a C-II controlled substance is necessary. The pharmacist can also assume the prescriber believes that no other alternative treatment is sufficient for the patient. If these two criteria are met, then an oral prescription for an emergency supply may be issued.

On receipt, the oral prescription must be immediately reduced to writing. The amount prescribed and dispensed for an emergency prescription may only be enough to last the patient through the emergency, up to 72 hours. This amount must be recorded.

Within 7 days, the prescriber must replace the emergency order with a written, signed hardcopy for the amount dispensed. The words "Authorization for Emergency Dispensing" must be written on the prescription. The date of the emergency prescription must also be included. If the prescriber fails to do this within 7 days, then the pharmacist must notify the DEA.

Prescribing C-III, IV, and V Products

A prescription for C-III, IV, and V controlled substances may be presented in either written form or orally.

When a verbal order is received, the pharmacist must immediately write down the information. However, unlike C-II controlled substance prescriptions, a written hardcopy from the prescriber is not required for C-III, C-IV, and C-V medications. The verbal order and the written copy serve as the original and may be filled and dispensed.

DISPENSING REQUIREMENTS AND RESTRICTIONS

Labeling Requirements and Exemptions

When a patient receives a prescription for a controlled substance, the label on the prescription vial must contain certain information. As stated, the FDCA listed four items required for all prescription vial labels. The CSA also lists required items, some of which are repeats from the FDCA and some of which are new. The CSA requires the following topics:

- The name and address of the pharmacy (same as the FDCA)
- The prescription number (same as the FDCA)
- The name of the prescriber (same as the FDCA)
- The date of the initial dispensing (FDCA said date of issuing or of filling)
- The date of refilling, if any (not an issue for C-IIs because they have no refills)
- The name of the patient
- Directions for use
- The statement "Caution: Federal law prohibits the transfer of this drug to any patient other than the patient for whom it was prescribed."

Labeling requirements are different for hospitals and nursing homes. Not all of the label information mentioned pertains to these institutions. Hospitals and nursing homes do not need to include all of this information, provided that

- Not more than a 7-day supply of a C-II controlled substance is dispensed
- Not more than a 34-day supply of C-III, C-IV, or C-V controlled substances is dispensed
- The drug is not in possession of the patient before administration
- The institution keeps appropriate records of inventory and administration

Dispensing C-II Products

When dispensing a C-II controlled substance in a retail pharmacy setting, a few extra rules must be followed.

C-II controlled substances are not refillable. There are no exceptions to this rule. A new written prescription must be obtained for any additional refills of a C-II controlled substance.

If the pharmacy is unable to fill the prescription for the entire amount requested, then a partial amount may be dispensed. This partial amount and the date must be written on the prescription face. The order must also be completed, or filled with the remaining amount, within 72 hours. If the order cannot be completely filled within the specified 72 hours, then a new prescription for the remaining quantity must be obtained from the prescriber. An exception to this is that prescriptions for patients in nursing homes and prescriptions for terminally ill patients may be partially filled as many times as needed for up to 60 days without obtaining a new prescription.

Dispensing C-III, IV, and V Products

The rules surrounding the filling of C-III, C-IV, and C-V controlled substances are not as strict as those rules surrounding C-II controlled substances.

The medications in these schedules are allowed to be refilled, although there are stricter rules for these drugs than for noncontrolled substances. C-III, C-IV, and C-V controlled substances may be refilled a maximum of five times. The prescription also expires 6 months from the day it was written whether the refills have all been used or not, compared with the standard 1 year for noncontrolled medications. These prescriptions are not allowed to be refilled with a larger quantity than initially prescribed.

If a pharmacy is unable to completely fill a prescription of C-III, C-IV, and C-V controlled substances, then the remaining quantity may simply be filled as soon as possible. No time restrictions are followed for these drugs other than the 6-month expiration time.

Limits on Products Containing Pseudoephedrine, Ephedrine, and Phenylpropanolamine

In an effort to enhance efforts at controlling the illegal manufacture of methamphetamine, the federal government now limits the sale of any OTC product containing pseudoephedrine, ephedrine, and phenylpropanolamine, similar to what many states have done in the past. The new federal law limits any individual person to no more than 3.6 g of any of these products per day and 9.0 g per 30 days. If the seller is a mail order pharmacy or "mobile seller" such as a kiosk in a mall or airport, then the 30-day limit is 7.5 g. All nonliquid forms must be in blister packs or other unit dose packets.

All sellers must keep these products behind a counter or in a locked cabinet and maintain a written or electronic log book containing a record of the purchaser's name and address, product name, quantity sold, and the date and time of each sale. The purchaser must show a photo ID and sign the log book entry.

The logbook and ID requirements do not apply to purchases of 60 mg or less of pseudoephedrine.

States that already have these regulations have seen huge reductions in illegal methamphetamine lab activity, although they also report huge increases in importation of illegal methamphetamine, mostly from Mexico.

Mailing Controlled Substances

The mailing of a controlled substance is allowed by the U.S. Postal Service (USPS), but the prescription vial (or inner container) must be properly labeled and securely sealed with a child-resistant cap. A mailing envelope (the outer container) must be placed over the inner container, and this outer container may bear no markings indicating that a controlled substance is inside the package. The USPS forbids the mailing of poisons, alcohol, and flammables.

Other delivery services such as UPS or FedEx have their own regulations.

Transferring Prescriptions and Refills between Pharmacies

The transferring of controlled substance prescriptions and refills applies only to those drugs in C-III, C-IV, and C-V. Because no refills are allowed for C-II drugs, a pharmacy will never transfer a prescription for C-II medications.

When transferring a prescription to another pharmacy, the transferring pharmacy must write "Void" on the face of the original prescription. The transferring pharmacy must also note several other items on the prescription:

- The name and address of the receiving pharmacy
- The date of transfer
- The DEA number of the receiving pharmacy
- The name of the receiving pharmacist

The pharmacy receiving the prescription must record all of the routinely required prescription information on a prescription blank. The word "Transfer" must be written on the top of the prescription, and several pieces of information relating to the original pharmacy's handling of the prescription must also be recorded:

- The original date of the prescription
- The date originally dispensed
- The number of refills originally authorized
- The date of the last refill
- The number of remaining refills
- The name and address of the transferring pharmacy
- The date of transfer
- The DEA number of the transferring pharmacy
- The name of the pharmacist transferring the prescription

By law, both parties must maintain these records for a period of at least 2 years.

REPORTING THEFT

Theft of a controlled substance is a matter that must be addressed. Any sort of theft — theft by a robber or burglar or theft by an employee — must be reported to the DEA, the state board of pharmacy, and the local police. Because controlled substances are inventoried, and any inspection will compare purchased amounts to inventory and dispensed amounts, a pharmacy must report thefts to be able to explain missing items to a potential DEA or state board of pharmacy inspector.

After the discovery of a theft, a DEA Form 106 must be filled out and sent to the DEA (see Appendix 5). The name and address of the pharmacy, the DEA registration number, the type of theft, and the amount of controlled substances stolen are all recorded on Form 106. Any local police who were notified of the theft and any internal store codes marking the containers must also be noted on DEA Form 106. Three copies of this form are filled out at once. The pharmacy retains one copy, and the other two copies are forwarded to the DEA. The particular state's board of pharmacy may also have additional reporting rules.

In the event these forms are lost or stolen, the registrant must immediately notify the DEA. If the serial numbers of the missing forms are known, then this information must be given to the DEA.

If the theft is thought to be a case of employee theft, then anyone with information of a fellow employee's action must report this information to a responsible security officer of the employer.

SAMPLE QUESTIONS FOR STUDENT REVIEW

1. What is a compounder pharmacy?
2. What are coincident activities regarding DEA registration?
3. When a pharmacy distributes as a coincident activity to its dispensing registration, how many controlled substance doses may it distribute in a year before having to get another registration as a distributor?
4. Which of the following people need to obtain personal DEA registration numbers, and which are covered by their employer's number?
   - Physicians
   - Physician's assistants
   - Pharmacists
   - Nurse practitioners
   - Dentists
   - Nurses
   - Pharmacy technicians
   - Licensed professional nurses
   - Veterinarians
5. If a pharmacy services both a hospital and a narcotic addiction treatment program, then how many different DEA registration numbers must it have? What if it also operates a retail community pharmacy?
6. Describe the ways a pharmacy may store its inventory of controlled substances.
7. Which control schedule (I, II, III, IV, or V) has the highest abuse potential?
8. What are the two ways a drug can be listed in more than one control schedule?
9. Which control schedule includes illegal drugs?
10. Which DEA form is used to order C-II drugs?
11. How does a pharmacy order C-III, C-IV, and C-V drugs?
12. How does a physician order C-II drugs for an office supply?
13. How does a physician order C-III, C-IV, and C-V drugs for an office supply?
14. Which copy of DEA Form 222 is kept by the ordering party?
15. Which copy of DEA Form 222 is forwarded to the DEA?
16. Is a DEA Form 222 needed when pharmacies are just lending and borrowing C-II items?
17. Describe the three ways prescriptions may be stored in a retail pharmacy.

18. When does a C-II prescription require a red C stamp in the bottom right-hand corner?
19. Why is the red C stamp required at all?
20. When is the red C stamp not required at all?
21. How frequently must a pharmacy conduct an inventory of controlled substances?
22. Which controlled substance schedules require an exact count of doses on hand at the time of an inventory count?
23. How long must a pharmacy keep executed copies of DEA Form 222 filed on the premises?
24. Which C-V products may be sold as OTC drugs?
25. What is a midlevel practitioner?
26. Which letter begins the DEA registration number of a midlevel practitioner?
27. Which two letters may be the first digit of the DEA number of someone with full prescriptive rights, such as a physician or dentist?
28. How many numbers follow the letters in a DEA number?
29. Which of these DEA numbers could be valid: LS2473293; AS2473293; BP2473293?
30. For which types of medications may a dentist write prescriptions?
31. If you are aware that prescribers are writing for a drug they are not authorized to prescribe, then what should you do? What if you are unaware?
32. Under which two conditions may a hospital provide controlled substances to a person who is in an addiction treatment program? How long may each of these continue?
33. May a prescription for a controlled substance be pre-dated or postdated? What if it is for the patient's convenience?
34. When you receive an emergency oral prescription for a C-II product, how soon does the prescriber have to mail you a signed copy of the written Rx? How much medicine may be dispensed from this emergency oral C-II prescription?
35. List all of the items that must be included on the label of a controlled substance prescription vial.
36. When may a hospital or nursing home omit most of the above listed items on the label of a controlled substance?
37. How many times may a C-II Rx be refilled?
38. How many times may other controlled substance prescriptions be refilled?
39. How much time does a pharmacy have to completely fill a C-II Rx that was previously partially filled? What are the exceptions to this?
40. For how long is a C-IV prescription valid?

41. List all of the items that must be recorded by a pharmacy receiving a transferred C-III prescription.
42. List all of the items that must be recorded by a pharmacy receiving a transferred C-II prescription.
43. Which DEA form is used to report controlled substance theft?
44. Who must be notified of a controlled substance theft?

5

OTHER PERTINENT FEDERAL LEGISLATION

OVERVIEW AND OBJECTIVES

Pharmacy-specific legislation and regulations are not the only things we must adhere to in our daily practices. Everything from local business ordinances for retailers to accreditation requirements for institutions to simple public health issues also obviously affect us, making our profession a bit more involved and complicated than the average person's line of work.

Two of the federal issues that have great impact on us are the Health Information Portability and Accountability Act (HIPAA) and the Dietary Supplement Health and Education Act (DSHEA). Each of these has significantly affected our daily lives in many ways, and this chapter both outlines these laws and points out the positive and negative aspects as they have an impact on us.

Chapter 5 discusses the following subjects:

- An overview of the HIPAA requirements
- An analysis of the value of HIPAA to pharmacy and to each citizen
- An overview of the features of DSHEA
- An analysis of the impact of DSHEA
- Suggestions on how to provide quality products and services in light of today's regulatory climate

THE HEALTH INFORMATION PORTABILITY AND ACCOUNTABILITY ACT

History and Requirements

In 1996, HIPAA was passed by Congress to address several issues, such as ensuring that people can continue their health insurance or obtain similar coverage when they change or lose their jobs, reduce medical costs by standardizing information and reducing administrative costs, promote medical savings accounts, and protect patient privacy by establishing security standards. HIPAA mandates that health care institutions and businesses protect the privacy of the health information of their patients and clients. It outlines patients' rights to determine how their personal health information is used and to whom it is disclosed. It also requires that the privacy of this information is protected from inappropriate use.

Each individual health care provider, such as a pharmacy or a hospital or a clinic, must write a privacy policy and provide this to all patients. Also, all employees must be properly trained and have security clearance for only the level of information they need to do their jobs; for example, a physician would have clearance for all information, and a nurse's aide would have quite limited clearance.

No information should be shared with anyone who does not have a legal or ethical need for it. For example, if an emergency room, hospital, or clinic calls for a list of the prescriptions a patient is taking, then you should verify that it is indeed an emergency room, hospital, or clinic calling for a legitimate need. If you are convinced of the legitimacy of the request, then you should provide the information as a part of the person's proper care and document that you did so, including the identity of the caller and why you concluded that the call was a legitimate, legal request. To withhold the information because of privacy concerns could interfere with the person's care, leading to other legal issues. Another scene could include a patient's spouse or any other relative (including parent) or friend; you would need written permission to give out any information unless the person making the request is the legal guardian of the incapacitated patient or is the parent of a minor child.

States have different ages (some as young as 12) at which medical information becomes protected from parents, so you will need to be aware of your state's requirements. This becomes a trickier situation when the caller is someone other than the patient but the individual already has some knowledge of the patient's medications. It is legal to respond to things about which the caller has prior knowledge, so if the caller knows about the patient's medications, you can respond to what they already know as long as you do not expand on it. For example, if the caller asks,

"What heart medicine is my dad taking?" you should not give the information because they obviously do not know much about it, but if they
ask, "Which one of my dad's prescriptions, Medicine X or Medicine Y or
Medicine Z, is for the heart?" then they clearly have some knowledge of
the patient's health status and medications, so you can answer that specific
question. This point of someone having prior knowledge of some health
information also allows a friend or relative to pick up finished prescriptions
from a retail pharmacy as long as they identify themselves and sign for
the prescription. To come in and pick it up, they had to know it was
there, and that shows they have knowledge regarding that specific issue
of the patient's health information. If you have doubt regarding whether
to give out information, then refer the caller to your institution's release
of information department or to your supervising pharmacist.

Let us discuss some case study examples of situations and reasonable
actions. The solutions presented here are certainly not the only way to
deal with the situations, but merely reasonable points. You may think of
other points that could lead to interesting class discussions.

Case One

John Doe comes to your pharmacy and says he needs a list of his wife's
medications for insurance reimbursements. Mr. and Mrs. Doe are regular
clients of your pharmacy and are known to you. Should you give Mr.
Doe the list of Mrs. Doe's prescriptions? Assume that Mrs. Doe is not
mentally incapacitated, and therefore Mr. Doe is not her legal guardian.

Mrs. Doe's information is hers and hers alone. Mr. Doe may indeed
need a list for their insurance company, and his request may be perfectly
valid, but you really do not know that for sure. Maybe they are just about
to file for divorce, and he thinks her medication history will weaken her
case for custody of their children. You do not know, and it really does
not matter if you do because unless Mr. Doe is her legal guardian or has
power of attorney for Mrs. Doe's medical care (he would have legal
documents for this and give you copies), it is not up to anyone other
than Mrs. Doe to decide who sees her information. An easy and noncon-
frontational way around this problem would be to inform Mr. Doe that
your company policy is to run such lists after hours when the computer
is not so busy and to mail it the next day. If he wants to stop by and
pick it up the next day, then you would have to make up some story,
such as the list is printed by the wholesaler's server and mailed by them
automatically, or fall back on quoting the law and agreeing with him on
the hassle it causes everyone. It is better to quote the law and then get
on his side by agreeing with him on how foolish it is to make a person
go through all this inconvenience. Aside from the moral issues of telling

a "white lie," it is just plain easier to remember what you told him when you tell him the facts and the truth at the beginning. A well-known state governor was quoted as telling his staff always to tell the truth because "It's easier to remember what you said when you're questioned about it later." He was not concerned about the morality of it, just the fact that when you mislead someone, it is hard to remember exactly what you said or did, so it is fairly easy to get caught. The bottom line is that you cannot legally give this information to the spouse of a legally competent person, but you can inform the spouse of this without putting yourself in the position of the "information cop" simply by the way you phrase it.

Case Two

The telephone call in the first case comes to you at your practice in a local community hospital, and Mr. Doe wants to know about the medications given to his wife during her recent hospital stay so he can better understand the insurance statements.

Most institutions have a policy to deal with any information given to anyone other than the patient: the patient signs a form on admission listing the people that can be told about his or her care and condition, and a copy of this is kept with the patient's written records on the ward or in the file room as well as electronically. If you do not have the records (as would be typical of pharmacy staff) or do not want to take the responsibility of searching the electronic file for this form, then the caller should be referred to the hospital's release of information office, which can properly deal with it. Most hospital pharmacies have a policy of referring all information requests from outside sources to the release of information office. Your department should have this stated in the policies and procedures manual so there is no question regarding how to respond and so that you do not appear to be acting on your own. If it is a written department policy, then you have no choice in your response, and you will also have no involvement in the issue, which is by far the best position.

Case Three

A police officer comes to your pharmacy and wants to see the prescription information for Jane Doe. He is investigating an issue involving her and wonders if medication usage may have played a role.

Technically, the officer should have a search warrant allowing him access to this information, and you should not disclose records without seeing the warrant and making notes about it. In real life, many people would take the officer's word on this and allow him to look at a person's prescription profile without presenting a search warrant. Making photocopies of it might be a different matter, and these same people may then feel more comfortable with the force of a warrant to protect them. There are two reasons for the legal system using the search warrant procedure: it protects the rights of the defendant from overzealous police searches (and, yes, that does happen), and it protects the person who gives out the information from accusations of illegally disclosing private information. Police do not like hearing "no" when they ask for information, but you can cushion it by stating your complete willingness to help but explain that you want to be protected. Any competent police officer will understand your position. When he returns with a warrant, you are bound to cooperate fully within the confines of the warrant's scope.

Case Four

The police officer in the preceding case comes to your hospital pharmacy asking for the same information for the same reason. Just as in Case Two, the best policy is to refer him to your hospital's release of information office as directed by your department's policies and procedures manual and hospital policy.

All this may seem like splitting hairs and perhaps it is, but it is on such details that legal issues are followed or broken. We should keep the greater goal in mind in that keeping health care information private is really the proper thing to do, and each person should have the right to specify who should have access to this knowledge and what they do with it. You may think this goes too far in some cases, such as when an immediate family member is denied information on another's medications, but look at it this way: would a 60-year-old widower want his 35-year-old daughter to know that he has a prescription for Viagra and has been getting it refilled regularly? Would a 20-year-old unmarried woman want her father to know she has an active prescription for birth control pills? Would a person want someone else to know he or she has an active prescription for a breathing inhaler, glaucoma drops, an atypical antipsychotic, an antianxiety medication, a genital herpes treatment, or an antiviral commonly used for HIV? Perhaps a person would not mind the release of some of this information, but that is not for you or me to decide. Every mentally competent person should have control over his or her private information, whether it is banking records, salary level, or health information. You would not expect a bank to give out your financial information to someone without your permission, would you? You would not expect your supervisor or your institution's human resources department to give out your salary information without your permission, would you? The concept is the same.

Except for those with a legitimate legal or ethical need, it is your information, and you are the only one who should decide who knows it.

THE DIETARY SUPPLEMENT HEALTH AND EDUCATION ACT

The DSHEA was passed by Congress in 1994 as an attempt to bring regulation, standardization, and safety to the growing market for "natural" remedies such as herbs and vitamins. The legislation was only partially successful at this, mostly in response to a huge letter-writing campaign from citizens and businesses concerned that federal oversight would unreasonably limit their rights and choices in choosing pharmacological therapy. In addition, the limited requirements outlined by DSHEA have taken many, many years to implement and even then are not given adequate attention by the Food and Drug Administration's (FDA's) over-worked departments. However, there are many aspects of the law that are a great improvement over the past.

This law created a new category of pharmaceuticals to add to the previous prescription and over-the-counter (OTC) categories, that of a *dietary supplement*, which was defined as a product intended to supplement the diet and not intended as a cure for a disease and includes such ingredients as vitamins, minerals, amino acids, and herbs and other botanical products. The law also established a framework for safety of these products, including adherence to good manufacturing practices; limited claims and labeling regarding use and nutritional support; required ingredient labeling; and formed an Office of Dietary Supplements with the National Institutes of Health to examine the health claims of dietary supplements.

Implementation and definition of these features is not exactly straightforward with both the FDA and the industry responsible, leading to multiple interpretations and areas that are not adequately regulated.

Manufacturers must ensure that a product is safe before it is marketed but does not have to inform the FDA of their evidence if the product is a naturally occurring substance, even though the FDA is charged with the burden of proof of safety. A manufacturer must inform the FDA of what is referred to as a *new dietary ingredient* (anything not occurring naturally in foods) and its safety data 75 days before marketing it, but the FDA only keeps a record of this and does not verify it. You will recall that with OTC and prescription products, the FDA requires in-depth investigation into safety before marketing, as outlined in Chapter 3 . The DSHEA gives the FDA authority to enforce good manufacturing practices to emphasize a clean working environment in the manufacture and sale of dietary supplements, but these regulations were not finalized until December 2006 (at 12 years after passage of the law), and small firms have been given 3 to 5 years to implement them. In the meantime, they have been required to follow the requirements for food handling, which are less stringent than those for drug manufacture.

Label claims of effectiveness and usage are not verified by the FDA, but the manufacturer must have proof that they are truthful and not misleading and notify the FDA within 30 days of marketing the product. The effectiveness and usage claim may only refer to the product's effect on body function, nutrient deficiencies, or general well-being and may not claim to treat a disease. This can lead to interesting wording. For example, the label for saw palmetto may not claim to "treat symptoms of enlarged prostate," but it may claim to "improve men's urinary control." Red yeast may not claim to "reduce high cholesterol levels," but it may claim to "aid in promoting a healthy cardiovascular system." The differences in wording may sometimes seem silly, but that is how DSHEA deals with the lack of proof of effectiveness of these products.

Many questions about dietary supplements are a result of lack of scientific testing, which is a result of their very nature: first, a company cannot patent an herb or other plant or plant component, and companies are not willing to spend money on research on a product they cannot patent; also, there often are questions about which component of a plant is the active ingredient. As you can imagine, there are dozens of chemicals in any leaf, root, or bark of a plant, so which is the active ingredient, or is the activity a result of several chemicals blending together? This would take intense study, which is the role of the new Office of Dietary Supplements, which sponsors such studies. Periodically, the office publishes their latest findings on the safety and effectiveness of dietary supplements, providing solid information to compare with the folk tales that are the basis of most usage, even in Europe, where herbal products are commonly prescribed medications, even though their best information is usually an analysis of various folk tales and an estimation of their validity. Several items thought to be effective have been shown by new statistically valid studies to be no better than a placebo, so one is best served to treat all claims with a healthy dose of skepticism.

Even with the questions surrounding the marketing, sale, and use of dietary supplements, it is comforting to remember that most of them have an extremely mild side effect profile. In short, although they may not do you any good, they probably will not hurt you, either. The least that a pharmacy should do to best serve its clients is to know which herbals and other dietary supplements interact with OTC and prescription products and try to include these items in patients' medication profiles and to sell only products that have the U.S. Pharmacopoeia (USP) seal of verification. The USP is a nongovernmental organization that is recognized by the government as an official source of information and regulation. The USP tests dietary supplements for "identity, strength, quality, and purity" by examining their manufacture under existing good manufacturing practices and checking for accuracy in label ingredients and the amount each dose contains (they have found some products that had none of the ingredient advertised and others that had as much as 400% of the amount labeled) and for contaminants. Pharmacies should attempt to sell only those products that carry the USP's seal of verification when possible. Several of the more responsible manufacturers of dietary supplements work closely with the USP to provide the highest quality products possible; other manufacturers skirt the law, providing products of dubious quality. You are providing a service to your clients and limiting your legal liability when selling USP-verified products.

SAMPLE QUESTIONS FOR STUDENT REVIEW

1. If a person were to call your pharmacy and ask "What medicines does my mother take?" when would it be legal for you to answer?
2. If a person were to call your pharmacy and ask "What medicines does my child take?" when would it be legal for you to answer?
3. If a person were to call your pharmacy and ask "Which of these medicines is for my father's pain, X, Y, or Z?" would it be legal for you to answer? What could you tell the caller?
4. Is it legal for someone other than the patient to pick up finished prescriptions at a retail pharmacy?
5. What is a dietary supplement?
6. How safe are dietary supplements to use?
7. Can you recommend herbal products with full scientific confidence in your information?
8. What is the basis for most effectiveness and usage claims for dietary supplements?
9. Is it legal for a dietary supplement to be marketed as a treatment for migraine headaches?
10. What might be a legal way to phrase a claim that feverfew treats migraine headaches?
11. What is the best way to be confident in the quality of dietary supplement products?

6

ETHICS THEORY AND APPLICATION

OVERVIEW AND OBJECTIVES

Ethics and ethical behavior can be argued about endlessly, with most people making the point that ethics just comes down to doing what you think is right based on your own experiences, attitude, and judgment. Your personal viewpoint is formed throughout your life in deciding right from wrong and observing others making similar decisions and is influenced by parents, schools, and religion.

Your parents' impact is deep seated and often unrecognized, but the old saying, "The fruit doesn't fall far from the tree" is very true. Recognize it or not, like it or not, we all end up acting and thinking a lot like our parents did.

Schools educate not only to provide a method for personal development but also to support and maintain traditions of behavior. Education for personal development is an obvious thing; by taking the courses a school requires, you simply learn to think better. Why do you think they require all those math classes? Does anyone really need to know how to calculate the circumference of a circle or the length of one leg of a triangle very often? What about all of those formulas in algebra? How often do you use them? Almost never, but that is not the point of learning them. Math classes teach you how to solve problems in a way that improves your problem-solving skills in all aspects of life, which fulfills the school's goal of educating you to live a better life and be a better citizen. Maintaining traditions comes through the extracurricular aspects of school, such as music, sports, drama, and other group activities. Just attending school events gives us a sense of social validity and tradition, serving to help all of us just get along better with each other.

Religion is the one influence that comes to us tempered by centuries of thought, writings, and opinions. When you look into the history of many of today's religion-based attitudes and practices, you may be quite surprised at their origins and how they became influential today. Where did the idea of unmarried priests and nuns come from? Who chose which books to include in the Bible? Why do some people view pork as unfit to eat? Why do Amish and Hasidic Jews, as well as many others, wear only certain styles of clothing? Where did the method of choosing the Dalai Lama or the pope come from? Why do some religions have one god and others have several? Why do some religions go to great lengths to spread their message and convert others, and other religions go to great lengths to leave other people alone? What is each religion's official position on when life truly begins, and how did they reach that conclusion? Has is always been what it is today or has it changed over the centuries or even just the past decades? Today's religious beliefs are the result of hundreds and hundreds of years of examination, thought, and reflection based on the opinions of some of the greatest minds in history, but an individual person's religious beliefs are mostly influenced by where they were born and raised and what their parents believed. Very, very few people analyze all religions and then choose the one they want to belong to or make their own conclusions based on just their own analysis. For the most part, we all simply keep on following the same religion our parents did and believe what that religion's leaders tell us is right without thinking much about it. Even so, these religious beliefs are powerful influences on how we live our lives and what we think public policy should be, even for those who do not view themselves as very religious people. Religious attitudes pervade our actions and opinions in subtle, deep-seated ways that are far beyond the scope of this narrative.

Although all of this parental, scholastic, and religious discussion seems logical at first glance, it fails to take into account two other important considerations: the viewpoint of the society in which you live and the impact it has on developing your own view of what is right. Society's impact is easily shown by comparing two different standards of ethical behavior as seen in two different societies: the modern Western society of today and the ancient Roman society from roughly 500 B.C. to 1000 A.D. The ancient Romans held human life and rights in low regard, as seen in parents' treatment of unwanted children (they either killed them or sold them into slavery); the treatment of military prisoners (they either killed them or sold them into slavery); the treatment of conquered populations (those that resisted were either killed or sold into slavery); and the treatment of minorities (they were often controlled by feeding their leaders to the lions in exhibitions at the Coliseum in Rome and in hundreds of similar venues throughout the empire). Gladiators fighting to the death and the public slaughter of unarmed people by wild beasts were seen as a form of general entertainment, much as the audiences of today view sporting events, television, and movies. If modern-day Americans were to travel back in time to ancient Rome and try to point out to the citizens how barbaric and morally wrong they were in their treatment of other human beings, they would be met with blank stares because there would be no understanding of the concepts of human kindness and appropriate treatment. Their enjoyment of gladiator bouts and human sacrifice to wild animals would be no different from our enjoyment of Bach, Beethoven, the Beach Boys, or baseball and basketball.

It is easy to see how living in such a society would mold people's views of ethical behavior in ways that today's citizens would view as reprehensible, but the point to be made with this comparison is that, in the forming of ethical standards, it is impossible to escape the role played by the society in which one lives. Each individual's ethical behavior takes into consideration current social standards. Ethical standards of one society (today's, for example) and another (ancient Rome's, for example) may not agree, but people in each society are behaving ethically based on the standards of that society. One society may think that the other society's standards are wrong, but that opinion is based on the society that has formed the particular standards. Modern Americans may disagree with medieval witch burnings, the amputation of a thief's hands (which, by the way, is still practiced today in certain societies), stoning an adulterer to death, and crucifixion, but they all reflect the ethics of their time and society.

Study of the topic of ethics presents reference points of current proper behavior and decision making in today's society, reference points that will provide support when such things need to be decided. Society's values guide its citizens and carry more influence than the opinions of an individual person, an individual religion, or an individual school district and therefore provide public support for decisions. By having a working knowledge of ethical decision-making topics, individuals are equipped to make better-quality decisions with which others in the society will agree, making such choices defensible both legally and morally.

Chapter 6 discusses the following subjects:

- An overview of ethical decision making
- The development of medical ethical standards and codes of ethical behavior
- Ethical behavior in business and professional relationships
- Patient's rights
- Current issues and cases

THE DEVELOPMENT OF PHARMACEUTICAL ETHICAL CONSIDERATIONS

Ethics can be defined as both the science of human nature and a system of principles governing morally correct conduct. *Morality* is considered the confirmation of generally accepted standards of conduct.

These terms are often mistaken for one another because their definitions are so similar. Although their definitions are not exactly interchangeable or synonymous, it is relatively safe to assume that people cannot develop a system of ethics without first consulting their society's generally accepted standards of conduct. These standards of conduct and the resulting system of ethics are derived from a group's basic need to preserve its own society. By implementing guidelines, groups are better able to avoid conflict, upheaval among members, and disintegration of the group as a whole. In an ideal situation, ethics would come naturally — no disagreements or discrepancies would surface; everyone would hold essentially the same set of ideals to be true. But, because every person is not the same, these standards can vary among individuals even though they have been lifelong members of the same society. Something as simple as a slightly different interpretation of a society's values can greatly affect a person's belief. Ideally, everyone would share the same opinion — if most people are raised under the same set of values, then personal thoughts should not differ, should they? Unfortunately, ethics and the issues of morality surrounding ethics are not always as simple as right versus wrong.

Ethics cannot always be followed to the letter. Ethics can be divided into two main categories: consequential and nonconsequential. Consequential ethics place emphasis on the "correct" end result — the consequences of the act validate the action, and all actions should bring about the greatest good for the greatest number. Nonconsequential ethics place emphasis on truth. Ethical issues are viewed as right or wrong. The outcome is not the most important issue. The most important issue is the action that brought about the outcome. Obviously, a large gray area separates these two extremes, and most people's views fall somewhere between the two. Without clearly defined ethical rules, society's decision making becomes more complicated.

Within society, groups (e.g., religious, family, and professional groups) must all coexist. Often, a person belongs to more than one of these groups at the same time. At its core, each group holds to a set of collective values, and each of these groups may not adhere to the exact same set of standards as another. This could cause a dilemma for individuals who see the slight variations between the groups of which they are members.

Professions often form individual sets of standards to which they refer for guidance. For example, the best-known set of guidelines for a profession would most probably be the ancient Greek Hippocratic oath for physicians. The Hippocratic oath states:

I swear by Apollo the physician and Aesculapius, Hygeia and Panacea and all the gods and goddesses, that, according to my ability and judgment, I will keep this Oath and this covenant.

To reckon him who taught me this Art equally dear to me as my parents, to share my substance with him and relieve his necessities if required; to look upon his offspring on the same footing as my own brothers and to teach them this Art, if they shall wish to learn it, without fee or stipulation; and that by precept, lecture and every other mode of instruction, I will impart a knowledge of the Art to my own sons and those of my teachers and to disciples who have signed the covenant and have taken an oath according to the law of medicine, but no one else.

I will follow that system of regimen which, according to my ability and judgment, I consider for the benefit of my patients and abstain from whatever is deleterious and mischievous. I will give no deadly medicine to anyone if asked, nor suggest any counsel; and in like manner I will not give to a woman an abortive remedy. With purity and with holiness I will pass my life and practice my Art.

I will not cut persons labouring under the stone, but will leave this to be done by such men as are practitioners of this work. Into whatever houses I enter, I will go into them for the benefit of the sick and will abstain from every voluntary act of mischief and corruption; and further, from the seduction of females or males, or freemen and slaves.

Whatever, in connection with my professional practice, or not in connection with it, I see or hear, in the life of men, which ought not to be spoken of abroad, I will not divulge, as reckoning that all such should be kept secret. While I continue to keep this Oath unviolated, may it be granted to me to enjoy life and practice of the Art, respected by all men, in all times. But Should I trespass and violate this Oath, may the reverse be my lot.

CODE OF ETHICS BACKGROUND AND PROGRESSION

Codes of ethics for other medical professions also exist. Although neither as old nor as familiar as the Hippocratic oath, guidelines for the profession of pharmacy have been found that date back to the 16th century. The 17th century brought about the forming of apothecary societies. It was not until the 19th century that pharmaceutical education was available in the United States.

The first college of pharmacy in the United States was the Philadelphia College of Pharmacy, which was founded in 1821. In 1848, the college adopted the nation's first pharmaceutical code of ethics. This code is the standard from which present-day codes have been derived.

The 1848 Philadelphia code of pharmacy states:

> Pharmacy being a profession which demands knowledge, skill and integrity on the part of those engaged in it and being associated with the medical profession in the responsible duties of preserving the public health and dispensing the useful though often dangerous agents adapted to the cure of disease, its members should be united on some general principles to be observed in their several relations to each other, to the medical profession and to the public.

> The Philadelphia College of Pharmacy being a permanent, incorporated institution, embracing amongst its members a large number of respectable and well-educated apothecaries, has erected a standard of scientific attainments, which there is a growing disposition on the part of the candidates for the profession to reach; and being desirous that in relation to professional conduct and probity, there should be a corresponding disposition to advance, its members having agreed upon the following principles for the government of their conduct:

> ■ 1st. The College of Physicians of Philadelphia having declared that any connection with, or monied interest in apothecaries' stores, on the part of the physicians, should be discountenanced; we in like manner consider that an apothecary being fully engaged in furthering the interests of any particular physician, to the prejudice of other reputable members of the medical profession, or allowing any physician a percentage or commission on his prescriptions, as unjust toward that profession and injurious to the public.

- 2nd. As the diagnosis and treatment of disease belong to the providence of a distinct profession and as a pharmaceutical education does not qualify the graduate for these responsible offices; we should, where it is practicable, refer applicants for medical aid to a regular physician.
- 3rd. As the practice of Pharmacy can only become uniform by an open and candid intercourse being kept up between apothecaries, which will lead them to discountenance the use of secret formulae and promote the general use and knowledge of good practice, and as this College considers that any discovery which is useful in alleviating human suffering, or in restoring the diseased to health, should be made public for the good of humanity and the general advancement of the healing art — no member of the College should originate or prepare a medication, the composition of which is concealed from other members, or from regular physicians. Whilst the College does not at present feel authorized to require its members to abandon the sale of secret or quack medicine, they earnestly recommend the propriety of discouraging their employment, when called upon for an opinion as to their merits.
- 4th. The apothecary should be remunerated by the public for his knowledge and skill and his charges should be regulated by the time consumed in preparation, as well as by the value of the article sold; although location and other circumstances necessarily affect the rate of charges at different establishments, no apothecary should intentionally undersell his neighbors with a view to his injury.
- 5th. As medical men occasionally commit errors in the phraseology of their prescriptions, which may or may not involve ill consequences to the patient if dispensed and be injurious to the character of the practitioner; it is held to be the duty of the apothecary, in such cases, to have the corrections made, if possible, without the knowledge of the patient, so that the physician may be screened from censure. When the errors are of such a character as not to be apparent, without the knowledge of circumstances beyond the reach of the apothecary, we hold him blameless in case of ill consequences, the prescription being his guarantee, the original of which should always be retained by the apothecary.
- 6th. Apothecaries are likewise liable to commit errors in compounding prescriptions — first, from the imperfect handwriting of the physicians; secondly, owing to the various

synonyms of drugs in use and their imperfect abbreviations; thirdly, from the confusion which even in the best-regulated establishments may sometime occur, arising from press of business; and fourthly, from deficient knowledge or ability of one or more of the assistants in the shop, or of the proprietor — we hold that in the first three instances named, it is the duty of the physician to stand between the apothecary and the patient, as far as possible; and in the last that he should be governed by the circumstances of the case — drawing a distinction between an error made by a younger assistant accidentally engaged and a case of culpable ignorance or carelessness in the superior.

■ 7th. As the apothecary should be able to distinguish between good and bad drugs, in most cases and as the substitution of a weak or inert drug for an active one, may, negatively, be productive of serious consequences — we hold that the intentional sale of impure drugs or medicines, from motives of competition, or desire of gain, when pure articles of the same kind may be obtained, is highly culpable and that it is the duty of every honest apothecary or druggist to expose all such fraudulent acts as may come to his knowledge. But in reference to those drugs which cannot be obtained in a state of purity, he should, as occasion offers, keep physicians informed as to their quality, that they may be governed accordingly.

■ 8th. As there are many powerful substances that rack as poisons, which as constantly kept by apothecaries and pre-scribed by physicians and which are only safe in their hands, as arsenious acid, vegetable alkaloids, ergot, cantharides, etc. — we hold that the apothecary is not justified in vending these powerful agents indiscriminately to persons unqualified to administer them and that a prescription should always be required, except in those cases when the poisons are intended for the destruction of animals or vermin — and in these instances only with the guarantee of a responsible person. And we hold that when there is good reason to believe that the purchaser is habitually using opiates or stimulants to excess, every conscientious apothecary should discourage such practice.

■ 9th. No apprentice to the business of apothecary should be taken for a less term than four years, unless he has already served a portion of that time in an establishment of good character. Apprentices should invariably be entered as

matriculants in the school of pharmacy and commence attendance on its lectures at least two years before the expiration
of their term of apprenticeship; and as the progress of our
profession in the scale of scientific attainment must depend
mainly upon those who are yet to enter it — it is recommended that those applicants who have had the advantage
of a good preliminary education, including the Latin language,
should be preferred.

In 1852, the American Pharmaceutical Association member Henry P.
Hynson drafted a code of ethics for the Maryland Pharmaceutical Association. This "new" code of ethics was a decidedly more in-depth code of
ethics than the previous code. Hynson's code of ethics took into account
the complex relationships and other avenues in which pharmacy as a
profession was involved. A major point of interest in Hynson's code of
ethics was respect. Hynson addressed the respecting of the pharmacist
himself. He believed that pharmacists should be thoroughly qualified to
fulfill the everyday requirements called for as a pharmacist.

Hynson's first element of respect was that a pharmacist should possess
good moral character. Addiction to abusive drugs and the reliance on
alcohol are not allowed. Pharmacists should do all they can to continue
to educate themselves. In addition to education, the pharmacist should
recognize the standards set by both the *U.S. Pharmacopeia* and the
National Formulary for the Articles of Materia Medica.

The second point of interest regarding respect deals with respecting
the pharmacist's relations with those from whom he makes purchases.
The point of this section of the code was to promote fair dealing between
pharmacists and their suppliers. Honesty and integrity were valued in
commerce between the two. Pharmacists also were to follow all trade
rules and regulations.

The third point of interest regarding respect concerns respect between
pharmacists. Hynson's code of ethics follows the adage "do as he would
be done by." Pharmacists would not in any way discredit another pharmacist for their own gain.

The fourth avenue of respect in the profession of pharmacy concerns
respecting the unique pharmacist relationship with physicians. Pharmacists
should not substitute ingredients without the consent of the physician,
and with the drafting of this specific code of ethics, pharmacists were
instructed not to place copies of the physician's prescriptions on the
container unless the physician specifically instructed the pharmacist to do
so. Also, even if the patient requested directions, the pharmacist was not
to comply with that request. The pharmacist was instructed never to
discuss the physician's request with the "customer" for whom it was

intended. The composition of the prescription was also not to be disclosed to the recipient.

In 1870, the American Pharmaceutical Association revised and expanded a set of objectives it felt was noteworthy. The association wished to set the tone for the expanding world of pharmacy, and the new list of objectives was more far-reaching and comprehensive than previous efforts. The 1870 update addressed several points, many newly identified:

- To improve and regulate the drug market by preventing the importation of inferior, adulterated, or deteriorated drugs and by detecting and exposing home adulteration
- To establish the relations between druggists, pharmaceutists, physicians, and the people at large on just principles that shall promote the public welfare and tend to mutual strength and advantage
- To improve the science and the art of pharmacy by diffusing scientific knowledge among apothecaries and druggists, fostering pharmaceutical literature, developing talent, stimulating discovery and invention, and encouraging home production and manufacture in the several departments in the drug business
- To regulate the system of apprenticeship and employment to prevent, as far as practicable, the evils flowing from deficient training in the responsible duties of preparing, dispensing, and selling medicines
- To suppress empiricism (i.e., quackery) and to restrict the dispensing and sale of medicines to regularly educated druggists and apothecaries
- To uphold the standards of authority in the education, theory, and practice of pharmacy
- To create and maintain a standard of professional honesty equal to the amount of our professional knowledge, with a view to the highest good and greatest protection to the public

As strange and foreign as a few of these sections may appear to the modern-day pharmacist or pharmacy technician, the beginning of the modern ethical codes that are followed today can be seen.

It comes as no surprise that work in the medical profession comes with both pros and cons. Helping others is one of the main reasons numerous people join the medical professions, but with current technological advancements and the often-changing legal world, today's pharmacy professionals can often meet many confounding issues. Having standardized codes of behavior developed by recognized national organizations can be of great assistance with the day-to-day decisions on professional behavior that are faced.

In 1952 and 1969, the American Pharmaceutical Association revised its code of ethics, and in 1975, an amendment was made to the code. The present-day American Pharmaceutical Association Code of Ethics for Pharmacists was adopted by the group in 1994. Although this set of codes is an asset for the pharmacy professional, these amendments are not law. Each decision that a pharmacy professional must make needs to be fully measured against the ethical ramifications of that decision and the law.

AMERICAN PHARMACEUTICAL ASSOCIATION CODE OF ETHICS FOR PHARMACISTS

Pharmacists are health professionals who assist individuals in making the best use of medications. This code, prepared and supported by pharmacists, is intended to state publicly the principles that form the fundamental basis of the roles and responsibilities of pharmacists. These principles, based on moral obligations and virtues, are established to guide pharmacists in relationships with patients, health professionals, and society.

I. A pharmacist respects the covenantal relationship between the patient and the pharmacist. Considering the patient–pharmacist relationship as a covenant means that a pharmacist has moral obligations in response to the gift of trust received from society. In return for this gift, a pharmacist promises to help individuals achieve optimum benefit from their medications, to be committed to their welfare, and to maintain their trust.

II. A pharmacist promotes the good of every patient in a caring, compassionate, and confidential manner. A pharmacist places concern for the well-being of the patient at the center of professional practice. In doing so, a pharmacist considers needs stated by the patient as well as those defined by health science. A pharmacist is dedicated to protecting the dignity of the patient. With a caring attitude and a compassionate spirit, a pharmacist focuses on serving the patient in a private and confidential manner.

III. A pharmacist respects the autonomy and dignity of each patient. A pharmacist promotes the right of self-determination and recognizes individual self-worth by encouraging patients to participate in decisions about their health. A pharmacist communicates with patients in terms that are understandable. In all cases, a pharmacist respects personal and cultural differences among patients.

IV. A pharmacist acts with honesty and integrity in professional relationships. A pharmacist has a duty to tell the truth and to act with conviction of conscience. A pharmacist avoids discriminatory practices, behavior or work conditions that impair professional judgment, and actions that compromise dedication to the best interests of patients.

V. A pharmacist maintains professional competence. A pharmacist has a duty to maintain knowledge and abilities as new medications, devices, and technologies become available and as health information advances.

VI. A pharmacist respects the values and abilities of colleagues and other health professionals. When appropriate, a pharmacist asks for the consultation of colleagues or other health professionals or refers the patient. A pharmacist acknowledges that colleagues and other health professionals may differ in beliefs and values they apply to the care of the patient.

VII. A pharmacist serves individual, community, and societal needs. The primary obligation of a pharmacist is to individual patients. However, the obligation of a pharmacist may at times extend beyond the individual to the community and society. In these situations, a pharmacist recognizes the responsibilities that accompany these obligations and acts accordingly.

VIII. A pharmacist seeks justice in the distribution of health resources. When health resources are allocated, a pharmacist is fair and equitable, balancing the need of patients and society.

In addition, it is interesting to note that an oath for pharmacists exists. Like the Hippocratic oath of the physician, this oath of a pharmacist strives to maximize the potential a pharmacist can contribute.

Oath of a Pharmacist

- At this time, I vow to devote my professional life to the service of all humankind through the profession of pharmacy.
- I will consider the welfare of humanity and relief of human suffering my primary concerns.
- I will apply my knowledge, experience and skills to the best of my ability to assure optimal drug therapy outcomes for the patients I serve.
- I will keep abreast of developments and maintain professional competency in my profession of pharmacy.
- I will maintain the highest principles of moral, ethical and legal conduct.
- I will embrace and advocate change in the profession of pharmacy that improves patient care.
- I take these vows voluntarily with the full realization of the responsibility with which I am entrusted by the public.

In 1996, the American Association of Pharmacy Technicians realized the need for a code of ethics separate from that of the pharmacists. The association then drafted its own version of the code of ethics for pharmacy technicians.

Because pharmacy technicians' job duties and requirements differ from those of pharmacists, it is important for pharmacy technicians also to take into consideration their code of ethics.

AMERICAN ASSOCIATION OF PHARMACY TECHNICIANS CODE OF ETHICS FOR PHARMACY TECHNICIANS

Pharmacy technicians are health care professional who assist pharmacists in providing the best possible care for patients. The principles of this code, which apply to pharmacy technicians working in any and all settings, are based on the application and support of the moral obligations that guide the pharmacy profession in relationships with patients, health care professionals, and society.

I. A pharmacy technician's first consideration is to ensure the health and safety of the patient and to use knowledge and skills to the best of his/her ability in serving others.

II. A pharmacy technician supports and promotes honesty and integrity in the profession, which includes a duty to observe the law, maintain the highest moral and ethical conduct at all times, and uphold the ethical principles of the profession.

III. A pharmacy technician assists and supports the pharmacist in the safe, efficacious, and cost-effective distribution of health services and health care resources.

IV. A pharmacy technician respects and values the abilities of pharmacists, colleagues, and other health care professionals.

V. A pharmacy technician maintains competency in his/her practice and continually enhances his/her professional knowledge and expertise.

VI. A pharmacy technician respects and supports the patient's individuality, dignity, and confidentiality.

VII. A pharmacy technician respects the confidentiality of a patient's records and discloses pertinent information only with proper authorization.

VIII. A pharmacy technician never assists in the dispensing, promoting, or distributing of medications or medical devices that are not of good quality or do not meet the standards required by law.

IX. A pharmacy technician does not engage in any activity that will discredit the profession and will expose, without fear or favor, illegal or unethical conduct in the profession.

X. A pharmacy technician associates with and engages in the support of organizations that promote the profession of pharmacy through the use and enhancement of pharmacy technicians.

PHARMACY — A RESPECTED TRADITION

For a number of consecutive years, the profession of pharmacy has been ranked as the most trusted profession by the American people. Although consideration as the most trusted profession is most certainly commendable, it carries with it innumerable responsibilities — not only ethical but also legal. Sometimes, these responsibilities are easy to distinguish and carry out, but at other times, the area between ethics and the law, or between perceived right and wrong, becomes blurred.

Pharmacy professionals share many things in common. Education, career training, and a distinct sense of pride in their work are only a few. Excluding personal opinion, it can be safe to assume that the majority of people entering the pharmacy profession today share common goals and common professional values. Applying these values in challenging or difficult situations can test even the most patient pharmacy professional. Living up to the title of the most trusted profession comes with its own set of duties, especially when outside groups such as the federal government and pharmaceutical companies push agendas that have the potential — whether intentional or not — to add even more ethical dilemmas to the pharmacy profession.

Years ago, pharmacy's main job was the dispensing and compounding of drugs. Because of this relatively limited duty, ethical issues in the workplace were not as prevalent as they are today, and the law or the following of the law was the most important factor to consider. Today, in addition to dispensing and compounding medication, pharmacists counsel patients on proper medication usage, potential side effects, and drug interactions. Pharmacists also must be the mediator if and when questions arise with the patient or the prescriber. Because of the pharmacy professional's close personal contact with the public, problems can arise, and ethical applications may need to be considered.

With high standards firmly in place and competent professionals, the pharmacy profession will continue to excel and live up to its stellar reputation. The profession has proved through changing times that it can rise to the occasion and handle ethical and legal considerations.

PHARMACY-RELATED RELATIONSHIPS

In recent years, major emphasis has been placed on the pharmacy profession's ability to communicate effectively to and between patients, physicians, and other medical professionals and personnel.

No longer is dispensing medications pharmacy's only job. Its outreach now expands into the realms of improving patient outcomes by establishing long-term relationships with medical practitioners, patients, and other pharmacy professionals.

Each of these relationships is unique and warrants discussion. In a world that relies heavily on interpersonal interaction, one must take into consideration the level of professionalism needed to handle these sometimes-complex relationships.

Pharmacy Personnel-to-Personnel Relationships

Although one pharmacist's opinions about specific issues may differ from another's, major topics such as patient care, ethical considerations, and good practice standards are usually agreed on.

The simplest rule one can adhere to in the pharmacy personnel-to-personnel relationship is simple: treat others the way you wish to be treated. All people have their own opinions, and each is valid and to be respected. Treating each other with common courtesy and common sense automatically imparts respect for others as professionals and as simple human beings. People would all do well to conduct their professional and personal lives based on that simple adage: common courtesy and common sense.

Business practice questions can arise in a pharmacist-owned retail setting, and budget considerations can arise in institutional settings, but it is important not to let these financial matters cloud judgment on the pharmaceutical level. Different views of situations should not overshadow one fact: these professionals must remember that their patients and those patients' care are their number one priority.

Pharmacy Personnel–Physician-Provider Relationship

Pharmacists, pharmacy technicians, and physicians are all medical professionals who should rely on respect and honesty when dealing with one another. The patient's health care is the most important issue that must be focused on in this specific relationship.

Today's pharmacist–physician-provider relationship has evolved into a hands-on proactive practice in which the balance among proper diagnosis, proper utilization of medications, and proper monitoring parameters has further linked the professions of pharmacy and medicine.

In the past, the pharmacy field was often viewed by the medical profession as more of a business than a viable medical career. Pharmacy's advancement into patient care, mandatory patient medication counseling, and drug regimen monitoring has elevated the profession to a rightly deserved level. In some specific situations, pharmacists are now able to confer with a physician or other health care professional and, on diagnosis, prescribe medication for a patient's condition. With the health care provider and the pharmacist acting as a team, patients are better served because knowledge is collectively drawn from two specific areas of expertise.

With this combination of patient care and the application of mutual trust and respect, the pharmacist–physician-provider relationship will continue to have an impact in the area that most requires it: proper patient care.

Pharmacy technicians are the ones who allow this to occur. To concentrate on this interaction with physicians and other providers, the pharmacist must know that all other aspects of the pharmacy's operation are handled appropriately. Pharmacy technicians must realize that it is this trust between them and pharmacists that allows pharmacists to fully engage in patient care.

Pharmacy Personnel–Patient Relationship

Of any of the mentioned relationships, the pharmacy personnel–patient relationship is the most intimate and complex. To function properly, the pharmacist–patient relationship requires the maintenance of a delicate balance. Today's patients are realizing that pharmacy workers are professionals trained to handle medication questions and problems. Pharmacists and technicians are held in high esteem by the general public because of their roles in patient education, wellness, and healthy lifestyles. The trust extended by the public is a result of decades of service.

Today's pharmacy professionals must also take into consideration extraneous factors affecting everyday practice. Often, people select community retail pharmacies based on the level of convenience they offer. Many people select a pharmacy based on the distance between the pharmacy and their home or office, which is convenient because of the location. But, what happens when a person needs a prescription filled quickly and is away from the home or office and nowhere near his or her chosen pharmacy? Usually, the prescription will be filled at the pharmacy that is closest at the time of need. This may lead to utilizing the services of numerous pharmacies, a dangerous practice because of the lack of complete medication records at any one pharmacy, opening the patient to the risks of polypharmacy (unintended multiple drug orders to treat the same problem) and drug interactions. Others choose to fill their prescriptions based solely on price. Again, this practice may lead to utilizing the services of many pharmacies.

Although patients are completely free to choose the pharmacy or pharmacies of their liking, questions arise: What role do pharmacies play as a business? What roles do pharmacies play in properly servicing patients medically? The area between these two extremes is vast. Although a pharmacy most certainly is a business, at what point does the business aspect become completely secondary to the patients' health and well-being?

Even though the answer should be that the health and well-being of the patient are always the top priority, the answer to this is not always so easily found. Pharmacists and pharmacy technicians must do their absolute best to ensure that the patient's health care is of the utmost importance. This means cooperating with the pharmacy down the street, where "your" patients have been going because their prices are slightly lower than yours. This means cooperating with many different physicians, nurses, physician's assistants, and other health care providers to consolidate and organize your patient's medication regimen.

The professional relationships that a pharmacist or pharmacy technician develops with all those he or she may come into contact in the course of daily work is the fundamental basis for a successful pharmacy practice.

COMMUNICATING PROFESSIONALLY IN AN INFORMATION AGE

Years ago, prescription information and medication information were routinely concealed from the patient. Names of medications, dosage strengths, and instructions on how to properly use the medication were essentially kept a secret. The informative age in which we live today has drastically changed the way that pharmacists and pharmacy technicians communicate with others — especially patients.

Today, physicians, health care providers, pharmacists, and pharmacy professionals are not the only sources patients and the general public turn to when they have questions regarding drug therapy. Because of the overabundance of information — be it correct or incorrect information — now available, it is important that pharmacy professionals fully grasp the impact of proper, efficient communication with patients.

To ensure proper communication, many avenues need to be explored. Communicating effectively has long been a hallmark of the modern pharmacy practice. Keeping in mind the patients' health and well-being and taking the necessary measures to ensure it are an important consideration in the profession of pharmacy. Implementing the techniques necessary to communicate properly begins the moment a patient walks through the pharmacy's door. As patients ask a question or hand the pharmacy professional a prescription, they not only are soliciting a service but are also expressing their implicit trust in the pharmacy professional.

Informed consent is the idea of the patient freely consenting to receive medical treatment, including drug treatment. Pharmacists and pharmacy technicians often see new patients — patients with medical and medication histories that are unfamiliar to you. In cases such as these, it is of the utmost importance to gather as much information from the patient as possible. Also, when filling prescriptions for these new patients, one should never assume which disease state the medication is to treat. To make sure that the patients have indeed given informed consent to be treated with certain medications, the patient should be asked, "What are you using this medication for?" Keep in mind that the patient needs to be directly asked this question. A pharmacy professional should never assume that a medication is used to treat a certain condition; the patient should always be asked.

For example, if a patient came into a pharmacy with a prescription for amitriptyline, the pharmacist or pharmacy technician should never refer to it as a medication for depression. The patient should instead be asked, "What are you using this medication for?" If patients were indeed using the amitriptyline as a preventive measure against migraine headaches and were told the medication was primarily an antidepressant, then they might refuse the drug because they are "not depressed" or do not want to be treated with an antidepressant — a class of drugs that even today still carries a stigma.

In the day-to-day workings of a pharmacy, an odd struggle can be observed that pharmacists and technicians face. Often, pharmacists must choose how much information about potential side effects they should share with the patient, and technicians must decide how much information they can provide before calling for the pharmacist. All are faced with the dilemma of deciding how much information to disclose to patients. Some pharmacists believe that disclosing complete information would lead to noncompliance, and that selectively sharing information regarding adverse events would lead to better patient compliance. Others feel that patients are entitled to know everything about their medications and health conditions, with the idea that an informed patient can make better-quality decisions about their health care. Most pharmacists attempt to balance these two, and pharmacy technicians must form their own opinions surrounding this struggle.

Another service that is an integral part of pharmacy is the monitoring of patient drug therapy for duplications, allergies, and other complicating factors. Compounding this issue is the fact that many patients may fill prescriptions at several pharmacies. Patients should always be asked to list all the medications they are taking regardless of where they had their prescription filled. This practice will help to ensure proper monitoring and patient safety.

Although patient safety is of the highest importance, unfortunately mistakes are made from time to time. Although not intentional, these mistakes can place a patient in harm's way. When a mistake has been made, it is pertinent for all involved — the pharmacist, the pharmacy technician, and the patient — to come together and work through what potentially could be a difficult time. Acknowledging that a mistake has been made is the first step. One should never even consider covering up an error or deceiving others. By admitting to an error without hesitation, pharmacists not only establish themselves as persons of honor and high character, but also ensure they are doing the right thing for the affected patient. Interestingly, patients almost always appreciate such honesty and think better of the professional for it. Discussing problems the error may have caused and attempting to rectify the situation are the next steps that should be taken. Finally, measures need to be taken to prevent more mistakes from happening in the future. This can range from additional training for the involved employees if inadequate knowledge and skills were the cause, to changing the way things are done in the pharmacy's operation, such as relocating easily confused products or changing the workflow process.

Because the patient relationship with pharmacists and pharmacy technicians is based on trust, maintaining this trust is a top priority. Maintaining patient confidentiality is a duty that all pharmacy providers must observe. Sometimes, though, patient information must be shared with others. For instance, when a pharmacy professional calls a doctor's office and requests an authorization for a refill, the request information must sometimes be left with a nurse or a doctor's receptionist. Does this constitute breaking a confidence? Personal opinion aside, sharing "sensitive" information with the intent of helping the patient is not usually considered to be breaking a confidence. If this information were to be shared with unauthorized personnel, then this would be considered to be breaking a confidence.

As stated, maintaining patient trust should be taken seriously by both pharmacists and pharmacy technicians. The patient's welfare is the number one priority.

PATIENT'S RIGHTS

Medical care has, for centuries, focused on providing the best care for the patient, but in the past, the physician was relied on to make all decisions on behalf of the patient. Modern thinking has evolved so that now it is believed to be best when patients are as fully informed as possible and take an active role in decisions involving their medical care choices. There is a broad range represented in the phrase "as fully informed as possible," which varies with the patients' ability to comprehend, their level of education, and the physician's communication skills. In an effort to spell out guidelines that would standardize the approach to these issues and provide guidance for providers and hospitals when they are faced with dilemmas, the American Hospital Association (AHA) adopted a patient's bill of rights in 1972, which they later refined into today's statement, "The Patient Care Partnership."

American Hospital Association's Patient Care Partnership

The AHA's "Patient Care Partnership" is a brochure available to all hospitalized patients outlining what they should expect during care as an inpatient. Although it has several headings, such as "High Quality Hospital Care" and "A Clean and Safe Environment," perhaps its most significant portion is "Involvement in Your Care," which covers the most important aspects of hospitalization:

- Discussing your medical condition and information about medically appropriate treatment choices
- Discussing your treatment plan
- Getting information from you
- Understanding your health care goals and values
- Understanding who should make decisions when you cannot

By addressing these vitally important topics, the AHA establishes a standard of communication and conduct that should be expected.

Pharmacists and pharmacy technicians often interact with the patient on a level that is different from that of a physician or other medical professional provider. Numerous states have adopted sets of rights for the patient in a pharmaceutical setting. Although these rights may vary slightly, the basic idea is the same. Some common characteristics include providing professional care in a timely manner from a competent provider without regard to gender, race, age, or religion. All patients are to be treated with dignity. All decisions relating to drug therapy should be made with the patient's best interest in mind, and the pharmacists will do all they can to cooperate fully with the providing medical professionals. Pharmacy patients are also provided with patient drug monitoring, screenings for adverse drug reactions, and patient counseling. These "rights" provide the patient with freedom of choice based on becoming fully informed. They also should guarantee professional care.

Another aspect of medical law and patient's rights involves informed consent. Previously touched on briefly, informed consent and its associated ideas are discussed here in greater detail.

Informed consent falls under negligence law or medical malpractice. Informed consent focuses on the idea that it is individuals' fundamental basic right to control or make decisions about their bodies. This right can be withdrawn only under exceptional circumstances. Informed consent includes the right to accept or reject medical treatment, and the physician or other medical provider must obtain consent before any medical treatment is performed.

Individuals must understand the nature and the consequences of the procedure or treatment they are about to undergo. Patients who are able to comprehend this are considered mentally competent patients. Patients are presumed competent unless a reason is given to believe otherwise, such as an injury that affects mental stability or previous guardianship actions, for which other persons are legally responsible for people who are incapable of caring for themselves and making proper decisions. Someone else must then give consent for these patients.

In most cases, people under the age of 18, the legal age of consent, are deemed incompetent. People determined by the court to be incompetent are thought to lack the ability to make rational medical decisions. In these cases, someone known as a conservator is appointed for them. Elderly patients with decreased or limited mental function usually do not require court intervention. These patients can usually be deemed incompetent by their physician, and consent must be obtained from a third party.

This other party is often referred to as the surrogate decision maker. For example, when a patient is under the age of 18, the surrogate decision maker is usually a parent or legal guardian. In other cases, the surrogate decision maker can be an adult appointed by the patient through the law or a power of attorney for health care, a person selected by the court, or the nearest relative.

Physicians have a duty to disclose enough information to patients or their representatives about possible medical treatment so they can make an informed decision whether to undergo the procedure or the proposed treatment. The nature of and the reason for the treatment, the risks and consequences of the treatment, and existing alternatives and the consequences that may occur if the treatment is refused — all must be disclosed to patients before beginning any treatment.

Informed consent is usually documented in writing and signed by patients or their representatives. As always, a few exceptions to the rules exist. The duty to disclose does not extend to the performance of minor procedures. When a minor procedure is to be performed, patients sign admission forms that authorize the hospital to provide the necessary care.

The most distinct exception to the disclosure rule concerns emergency situations. In any situation when patients are not able to communicate (e.g., they are unconscious), lifesaving treatment may be administered without their consent. If patients are able to communicate or other directives exist, then the emergency exception does not apply.

When patients choose to stop or waive an informed consent discussion based on their belief that a physician knows best, this waiver of informed consent must, like all obtained consent, be documented in the patients' records.

In some instances, patients have made decisions ahead of time in the event they might be unable to make these decisions later for themselves. These are referred to as *advance directives* or *living wills*. Living wills are often the handwritten wishes of competent patients listing the measures they wish to have or have excluded in the event they are unable to make that decision later. This living will must comply with state standards, or it is not legally binding.

On the other hand, advance health care directives are more formal typewritten documents that comply with the state's requirements.

Informed consent is a powerful right and should be treated seriously. Legally and ethically, patients have the right to accept or refuse medical treatment. By law, these individual opinions must be respected, although court action can be taken to force people to accept treatment for themselves or those for whom they have guardianship. Most commonly, competent people who make decisions for themselves are not forced by a court to accept treatment against their wishes, even if their decision is a medically dangerous one. In the rare instance when a court intervenes, it is usually in a parental or guardianship situation when the patient will be greatly harmed by the parent or guardian's decision. This has been seen rarely in cases of people with extreme religious or other beliefs that limit medical assistance. Medical personnel as well as the courts are extremely reluctant to impose their will or judgment over the wishes of the patient or of the parent or guardian.

MODERN CONTROVERSIAL ISSUES

As discussed, ethics applied in the medical field are broad subjects that can be approached from numerous angles. The bottom line is that ethics help professionals do the right thing when presented with a moral dilemma.

Moral beliefs are ideas about right versus wrong, and not every person, culture, or society believes exactly the same thing. When moral beliefs clash, a moral dilemma occurs. Two good moral ideas are brought up against one another, and a conflict arises: which moral is the right moral?

To help solve a moral dilemma, ethics or ethical beliefs should be consulted. When faced with a moral dilemma and in deciding what to do, pharmacists rely on ethics.

It is never easy to be faced with an ethical dilemma. Ethical dilemmas in the medical field, or *bioethics*, present an even more disturbing problem because the situation often involves encounters that can alter or harm a patient's health. Numerous principles have been determined to be pertinent to the medical fields. When a person is presented with an ethical dilemma, these four primary principles provide guidance:

1. The first point is autonomy and respect for autonomy. *Autonomy* literally means self-governance or the ability to function independently. Application of this term to medical ethics regards respecting patients' decisions about what they feel is in their best interest. Regarding autonomy, patients have the right to know the risks and benefits of a medical treatment and the right to accept or refuse such treatment.

2. The second principle is beneficence. *Beneficence* means to be kind and to do good. In the medical ethics sense, beneficence can be applied to the measures one takes to help the patient's situation and make it better.

3. Nonmaleficence can be viewed as the matching side to beneficence. *Nonmaleficence* means to do no harm. It is obvious that health care professionals should not harm their patients through their actions, but they should also take into consideration the outcomes of their actions and ensure that the possible outcomes also do not harm the patient.

4. The fourth principle for medical professionals to observe is justice. *Justice* means treating everyone fairly. This principle is as simple as that.

Practicing in Both Legal and Ethical Senses

Ethical problems in the medical field are not always easy to solve. Although both systems of law and ethics are designed to protect and help individuals in society, it is important to note that law and ethics are not to be confused with one another. They might appear to overlap in meaning, but law and ethics are not the same things. What is ethical may not be legal; and what is legal may not be ethical. Balancing both of these systems is a vast undertaking.

Ethical Behavior in the Pharmacy Workplace

Every day, be it in a hospital, a community retail setting, or a nursing home, pharmacists and pharmacy technicians have the potential to be faced with ethical dilemmas. Educators in professional programs now realize the need for classes on ethics to be included in both pharmacy and pharmacy technician curriculums. These professionals need proper education to fall back on when a difficult situation presents itself.

When one is faced with a situation that presents an ethical dilemma, does a right way exist to solve the problem? Often, no "right" answers can be found, but by following a few guidelines and asking a few questions, the ethical dilemma may be a bit more easily resolved.

1. When a person is first presented with an ethical dilemma in a pharmacy setting, pharmacists or pharmacy technicians should initially try to gather pertinent information. Getting all the information together at once can prepare them to apply it later.
2. Attempt to identify the problem. Determine if the problem can be narrowed down and pinpointed or if the problem is larger in scope and is made up of more than one dilemma.
3. Analyze the problem or problems and attempt to identify all feasible alternatives that can be taken to efficiently solve the dilemma.
4. After gathering information, identifying the problem or problems, analyzing the problem, and coming up with different paths that can be taken, pharmacy professionals need to choose a way to solve the dilemma.
5. After attempting to solve the problem, evaluating the steps taken can help determine if the individual would act the same way if faced with similar circumstances in the future.

When practicing in a profession, people have a responsibility to themselves to act ethically. By acting in a way that produces good for themselves, people in turn bring about good for others. By embracing this responsibility, they become accountable for not only which actions were taken but also the results of those actions. By applying these techniques in a professional setting, better professionals will be made, and better quality decisions and actions will result.

To act ethically, lifelong learning is a must. Although lifelong learning does not necessarily guarantee easy answers in ethical dilemmas, the knowledge gained may make decision making easier down the road. Continuing to learn also makes more competent professionals able to better serve their patients. Keeping up with professional issues by reading pertinent journals, discussing topics as they arise with colleagues, participating in professional organizations and their seminars and educational efforts, and by just reading local newspapers and learning the folly of people's ways will deepen a professional's insights into human nature and how to deal with it.

No medical profession today would be complete without the observation of a vast number of different ethical dilemmas. Although everything from the introduction of the abortion pill and the morning-after pill to the plethora of direct-to-consumer advertising has recently sparked both political and ethical debates, pharmacy professionals know that, with the continuing advancement of science, even more ethical dilemmas will be brought to the forefront.

The following cases will help students and professionals to reflect about these possible situations. Questions will be asked that do not have just one correct or even any correct answers. Discussion of these cases is highly recommended, and formulating other questions that may be suggested can further enhance the debate on pharmaceutical ethics.

Case One

Sally Johnson is a newly licensed pharmacist. She has accepted the position of "floater" pharmacist for a large national chain, filling in at various stores in her area when they are short-staffed. While Sally is working, a woman comes to the counter with an empty bottle. She politely asks Sally to refill the prescription while she shops the store.

Sally takes the bottle and brings the record up on the computer. She then notices that Mrs. Olson just received ninety 0.5-mg alprazolam tablets 4 days earlier, with the directions to take one tablet three times daily. On deeper inquiry, Sally realizes that Mrs. Olson has received that same prescription five times in 3 months. She decides this is odd. She then realizes that the same pharmacist has filled each refill.

Mrs. Olson returns to the pharmacy for her prescription. Sally asks the woman if she has any tablets left at home, to which the woman curtly replies, "I need that medication. If Dan were here, he would fill it."

Questions:

1. If you were Sally, what would you do? Why?
2. Does Sally have a right to be concerned about this woman's pattern of use?
3. Does Sally have a reason to report Dan to the manager?
4. Does Sally have an ethical basis for refusing to fill the prescription?

Case Two

Peter Johnson is your store's new pharmacy technician. As head technician, it is your responsibility to train Peter. After he completes his training, he is ready to work.

Bill Larson, a regular patient at your pharmacy, hands Peter a new prescription for phenelzine. You overhear him tell Peter that he stopped by the doctor's office on his way home from work because he "just hasn't been feeling like himself lately." Peter fills the prescription.

You know Mr. Larson has been taking a selective serotonin reuptake inhibitor (SSRI) that was prescribed by a different doctor for depression.

When Mr. Larson returns, you ask him if the doctor he saw today knows about his SSRI. Bill replies, "This was a quick visit — I guess I didn't mention it. That's okay though, I'm going to this doc now, so I'll just take what he wants me to. Had a disagreement with the other doctor. I don't like him too much anymore. Done with him. It's none of his business what I do now."

Questions:

1. In addition to having the pharmacist warn against such concurrent use, would you urge the pharmacist to contact Mr. Larson's prescribing physician? Both physicians?
2. What if Mr. Larson specifically asks you not to contact his old physician? Would you still do so under the guise of "doing no harm"?
3. Discuss the steps you would take to help you arrive at your decision.
4. What alternatives exist in this case?

Case Three

Jim Hanson is the supervising pharmacist for a small local pharmacy. He is an active member of the community and knows most of the town's people.

One Saturday morning, Jenny, the 16-year-old daughter of a member of Jim's church choir presents him with a prescription for birth control tablets. She asks Jim not to run the prescription through the family's insurance plan. She simply wants to pay cash for the contraceptives.

Jim fills the prescription and, on dispensing the medication, finds out that Jenny has not told her parents about the birth control prescription.

Jim is concerned that a 16-year-old is receiving oral contraceptives without her parents' knowledge. Jim wishes to tell Jenny's father about her birth control pills but questions whether he should.

Questions:

1. If Jim were to tell Jenny's parents about the birth control pills, would he be breaking her confidence? Or, because Jenny is a minor, do her parents have the right to know, even without her consent?
2. Do you think it would make a difference if Jenny were 18? 13?
3. If Jenny had presented a prescription for something other than birth control pills, do you think Jim would have done the same?

Case Four

Mrs. Williams is a regular patient at a pharmacy. She is a rather nervous lady and always has numerous questions about the potential side effects and adverse reactions of her medications. On more than one occasion, she has refused medication based on the store's customary printout for the drug.

Today, she hands Bill, the pharmacy technician, a prescription for metoprolol.

Bill knows that Mrs. Williams has high blood pressure and often stops her medications because she is nervous about the side effects. He fills her prescription and "forgets" to include the patient printout describing potential side effects and adverse reactions. Bill's pharmacist instructs her on how to take her medication properly, and she then leaves the pharmacy.

Questions:

1. Do you believe withholding information would harm the patient? Benefit the patient? Both?
2. Would you have done the same as Bill did, or would you have included the information believing she would not take the medication on reading the information?
3. What else could have been done in this situation?

Case Five

Bob is the pharmacy manager. He has been working at this particular store for nearly 25 years. Linda is the newly hired pharmacy technician and has heard that Bob has certain ideas about running a business, and he does not like to be questioned.

On her first day at work, Linda observes some practices that do not seem "right" to her. She brings this up to another pharmacist over lunch and is told "not to step on Bob's toes."

Still, Linda is upset by what she has heard about and seen — narcotic counts that are not correct and the redispensing of returned medication. She does not want to lose her job, but these situations really bother her.

Questions:

1. What would you do if you were in Linda's position?
2. Would you deal with the ethical or legal issues first?
3. If Linda said nothing, would she be held accountable if these practices were later exposed?

Case Six

Elizabeth Peterson brings a prescription bottle to the pharmacy where Cindy is employed as a technician. Cindy attempts to refill the prescription for an allergy medication. Although it goes through insurance, Cindy notices that the woman filled the prescription only 2 weeks ago for a medication that should have lasted 30 days.

Cindy asks the woman about this. Elizabeth tells Cindy that her young son appears to have the same symptoms as she does, so she has been giving him some of her medication.

Questions:

1. If you were Cindy, would you want the pharmacy to dispense the medication?
2. Is it ethical to dispense this medication knowing that it will also be used by someone for whom it was not prescribed?
3. Are there any legal issues surrounding this case?
4. What other steps can be taken in this situation?

Case Seven

Tom is a pharmacy technician employed by an independent pharmacy. His employer, also the owner of the business, teaches classes about smoking cessation four times a month. His classes are very popular and often have a waiting list.

Tom's only problem is that the pharmacy sells cigarettes at the front of the store. When he asks his boss about this, the boss replies, "A guy has to make a buck somehow."

Tom is astonished and feels this is bad practice.

Questions:

1. Even if this practice is legal, is it ethical?
2. What would you do in the situation?

3. Name another situation similar to this that might also be seen in a retail pharmacy setting.

Case Eight

Ted Thompson is a pharmacist and storeowner. He does not believe the holistic medicine's and herbal companies' claims about their products' potential medicinal value. Al, his pharmacy technician, fully agrees with him.

Nonetheless, Ted stocks these products because they carry a large markup, he makes a good profit from them, and they move quickly off the shelves.

Lydia Swanson, an elderly patient, has heard wonderful things about a holistic tonic Ted stocks. Mrs. Swenson is on a fixed income, but she truly believes that this $30 tonic can alleviate some of her osteoarthritis symptoms.

She brings a bottle of the tonic to the cash register near where Al is working and asks, "Do you think this stuff really works?"

Questions:

1. What would you do in this situation?
2. Does Lydia's fixed income play into your decision? What if she were wealthy?
3. Should Ted stock these products if he does not believe in their value?

Case Nine

It is 4:55 on Sunday afternoon. The pharmacy where Susan is working closes at 5:00.

A gentleman she does not recognize brings a bottle with a label for an antiseizure medication to her pharmacy.

The bottle is not from Susan's pharmacy. She attempts to contact the other pharmacy for a copy, but they are closed. On closer inspection, Susan realizes the bottle says the prescription is out of refills. She questions the customer, and he informs her he is completely out of the medication.

Questions:

1. List the steps you would take in this situation.
2. Are any ethical situations apparent in this case?
3. Would it make a difference if the prescription were not a maintenance medication?

SAMPLE QUESTIONS FOR STUDENT REVIEW

1. Compare and contrast ethics and morality.
2. What kind of societal need is met by moral standards and an ethical system?
3. Compare and contrast consequential and nonconsequential ethics.
4. What was the initial code of ethics from which modern codes were derived?
5. How recent is the latest American Pharmaceutical Association code of ethics?
6. How recent is the American Association of Pharmacy Technicians code of ethics?
7. What are the three primary groups of people with whom pharmacy personnel deal?
8. Briefly describe key points in the pharmacy professionals' relationships with each of these groups.
9. What are some pros and cons of complete disclosure of all drug information to a patient?
10. What is the first step to take when a mistake is made?
11. What are the next two steps?
12. What level of patient information does the AHA's patient's bill of rights spell out?
13. On what idea does informed consent focus?
14. Which concepts must a mentally competent patient understand?
15. How much information can be revealed about 16-year-old patients to their parents? 20-year-old patients?
16. How much information can be revealed about mentally competent adult patients to their spouses? To their adult children?
17. When do the courts intervene in an individual's right to accept or refuse medical treatment?
18. List and explain the four principles of ethics that help people deal with ethical dilemmas.
19. Give some examples of lifelong learning that can help pharmacy professionals develop and maintain ethical standards and practices.

Appendix One

ROSTER OF STATE BOARD OF PHARMACY EXECUTIVES

Alabama

Mitzi Ellenburg, Assistant to the Executive Director
10 Inverness Center, Suite 110
Birmingham, AL 35242
205/981-2280, fax 205/981-2330
mellenburg@albop.com
www.albop.com

Alaska

Sher Zinn, Licensing Examiner
PO Box 110806, Juneau, AK 99811-0806
907/465-2589, fax 907/465-2974
sher_zinn@commerce.state.ak.us
www.commerce.state.ak.us/occ/ppha.htm

Arizona

Harlan "Hal" Wand, Executive Director
4425 W Olive Ave, Suite 140
Glendale, AZ 85302-3844
623/463-2727, fax 623/934-0583
hwand@azsbp.com
www.pharmacy.state.az.us

Arkansas

Charles S. Campbell, Executive Director
101 E Capitol, Suite 218, Little Rock, AR 72201
501/682-0190, fax 501/682-0195
charlie.campbell@arkansas.gov
www.arkansas.gov/asbp

California

Virginia "Giny" Herold, Interim Executive Officer
1625 N Market Blvd, N219, Sacramento, CA 95834
916/574-7900, fax 916/574-8618
virginia_herold@dca.ca.gov
www.pharmacy.ca.gov

Colorado

Wendy Anderson, Program Director
1560 Broadway, Suite 1310, Denver, CO 80202-5143
303/894-7754, fax 303/894-7764
wendy.anderson@dora.state.co.us
www.dora.state.co.us/pharmacy

Connecticut

Anne-Christine Vrakas, Board Administrator
165 Capitol Ave, State Office Bldg., Room 147
Hartford, CT 06106
860/713-6070, fax 860/713-7242
Anne-christine.vrakas@ct.gov
www.ct.gov/dcp/site/default.asp

Delaware

David W. Dryden, Executive Secretary
Division of Professional Regulation
Cannon Building, 861 Silver Lake Blvd, Suite 203
Dover, DE 19904
302/744-4526, fax 302/739-2711
debop@state.de.us
www.dpr.delaware.gov

District of Columbia

Bonnie Rampersaud, Executive Director
717 – 14th St. NW, Suite 600
Washington, DC 20005
202/724-4900, fax 202/727-8471
graphelia.ramseur@dc.gov
www.dchealth.dc.gov

Florida

Rebecca Poston, Executive Director
4052 Bald Cypress Way, Bin C04
Tallahassee, FL 32399-3254
850/245-4292, fax 850/413-6982
MQA_Pharmacy@doh.state.fl.us
www.doh.state.fl.us/mqa

Georgia

Sylvia L. "Sandy" Bond, Executive Director
Professional Licensing Boards
237 Coliseum Dr.
Macon, GA 31217-3858
478/207-1640, fax 478/207-1660
slbond@sos.state.ga.us
www.sos.state.ga.us/plb/pharmacy

Guam

Jane M. Diego, Secretary for the Board
P.O. Box 2816, Hagatna, GU 96932
617/735-7406 ext. 11, fax 671/735-7413
jmdiego@dphss.govguam.net

Hawaii

Lee Ann Teshima, Executive Officer
P.O. Box 3469, Honolulu, HI 96801
808/586-2694, fax 808/586-2874
pharmacy@dcca.hawaii.gov
www.hawaii.gov/dcca/areas/pvl/boards/pharmacy

Idaho

Richard K. "Mick" Markuson, Executive Director
3380 Americana Terrace, Suite 320, Boise, ID 83706
208/334-2356, fax 208/334-3536
rmarkuson@bop.state.id.us
www.accessidaho.org/bop/

Illinois

Kim Scott, Pharmacy Board Liaison
320 W. Washington, 3rd Floor
Springfield, IL 62786
217/782-8556, fax 217/782-7645
PRFGROUP10@idfpr.com
www.idfpr.com

Indiana

Marty Allain, Director
402 W. Washington St., Room W072
Indianapolis, IN 46204-2739
317/234-2067, fax 317/233-4236
pla4@pla.in.gov
www.in.gov/pla/bandc/isbp/

Iowa

Lloyd K. Jessen, Executive Director/Secretary
400 SW 8th St., Suite E
Des Moines, IA 50309-4688
515/281-5944, fax 515/281-4609
lloyd.jessen@ibpe.state.ia.us
www.state.ia.us/ibpe

Kansas

Debra L. Billingsley, Executive Secretary/Director
Landon State Office Bldg., 900 Jackson, Room 560
Topeka, KS 66612-1231
785/296-4056, fax 785/296-8420
pharmacy@pharmacy.state.ks.us
www.kansas.gov/pharmacy

Kentucky

Michael A. Burleson, Executive Director
Spindletop Administration Bldg., Suite 302
2624 Research Park Dr.
Lexington, KY 40511
859/246-2820, fax 859/246-2823
mike.burleson@ky.gov
http://pharmacy.ky.gov

Louisiana

Malcolm J. Broussard, Executive Director
5615 Corporate Blvd., Suite 8E
Baton Rouge, LA 70808-2537
225/925-6496, fax 225/925-6499
mbroussard@labp.com
www.labp.com

Maine

Geraldine L. "Jeri" Betts, Board Administrator
Dept. of Professional/Financial Registration
35 State House Station
Augusta, ME 04333
207/624-8689, fax 207/624-8637
geraldine.l.betts@maine.gov
www.maineprofessionalreg.org

Maryland

La Verne George Naesea, Executive Director
4201 Patterson Ave
Baltimore, MD 21215-2299
410/764-4755, fax 410/358-6207
lnaesea@dhmh.state.md.us
www.dhmh.state.md.us/pharmacyboard/

Massachusetts

James D. Coffey, Interim Director
239 Causeway St., 2nd Floor
Boston, MA 02114
617/973-0950, fax 617/973-0983
james.d.coffey@state.ma.us
www.mass.gov/dpl/boards/ph/index.htm

Michigan

Rae Ramsdell, Director
Licensing Division
611 W. Ottawa, 1st Floor, PO Box 30670
Lansing, MI 48909-8170
517/335-0918, fax 517/373-2179
rhramsd@michigan.gov
www.michigan.gov/healthlicense

Minnesota

Cody C. Wiberg, Executive Director
2829 University Ave SE, Suite 530
Minneapolis, MN 55414-3251
651/201-2825, fax 651/201-2837
Cody.Wiberg@state.mn.us
www.phcybrd.state.mn.us

Mississippi

204 Key Drive, Suite D
Madison, MS 39110
601/605-5388, fax 601/605-9546
www.mbp.state.ms.us

Missouri

Executive Director
P.O. Box 625, Jefferson City, MO 65102
573/751-0091, fax 573/526-3464
pharmacy@pr.mo.gov
www.pr.mo.gov/pharmacists.asp

Montana

Starla Blank, Executive Director
PO Box 200513, 301 S. Park Ave, 4th Floor
Helena, MT 59620-0513
406/841-2371, fax 406/841-2305
dlibsdpha@mt.gov
http://mt.gov/dli/bsd/license/bsd_boards/pha_board/board_page.asp

Nebraska

Becky Wisell, Executive Secretary
PO Box 94986
Lincoln, NE 68509-4986
402/471-2118, fax 402/471-3577
becky.wisell@hhss.ne.gov
www.hhs.state.ne.us

Nevada

Larry L. "Larry" Pinson, Executive Secretary
555 Double Eagle Ct., Suite 1100
Reno, NV 89521
775/850-1440, fax 775/850-1444
pharmacy@govmail.state.nv.us
http://bop.nv.gov

New Hampshire

Paul G. Boisseau, Executive Secretary
57 Regional Dr.
Concord, NH 03301-8518
603/271-2350, fax 603/271-2856
pharmacy.board@nh.gov
www.nh.gov/pharmacy

New Jersey

Joanne Boyer, Executive Director
124 Halsey St., Newark, NJ 07101
973/504-6450, fax 973/648-3355
boyerj@dca.lps.state.nj.us
www.state.nj.us/lps/ca/boards.htm

New Mexico

William Harvey, Executive Director/Chief Drug Inspector
5200 Oakland NE, Suite A
Albuquerque, NM 87113
505/222-9830, fax 505/222-9845
william.harvey@state.nm.us
www.state.nm.us/pharmacy

New York

Lawrence H. Mokhiber, Executive Secretary
89 Washington Ave, 2nd Floor W
Albany, NY 12234-1000
518/474-3817 ext. 130, fax 518/473-6995
pharmbd@mail.nysed.gov
www.op.nysed.gov

North Carolina

Jack William "Jay" Campbell IV, Executive Director
PO Box 4560
Chapel Hill, NC 27515-4560
919/246-1050, fax 919/246-1056
jcampbell@ncbop.org
www.ncbop.org

North Dakota

Howard C. Anderson, Jr., Executive Director
PO Box 1354
Bismarck, ND 58502-1354
701/328-9535, fax 701/328-9536
ndboph@btinet.net
www.nodakpharmacy.com

Ohio

William T. Winsley, Executive Director
77 S. High St., Room 1702
Columbus, OH 43215-6126
614/466-4143, fax 614/752-4836
exec@bop.state.oh.us
www.pharmacy.ohio.gov

Oklahoma

Bryan H. Potter, Executive Director
4545 Lincoln Blvd., Suite 112
Oklahoma City, OK 73105-3488
405/521-3815, fax 405/521-3758
pharmacy@pharmacy.ok.gov
www.pharmacy.ok.gov

Oregon

Gary A. Schnabel, Executive Director
800 NE Oregon St., Suite 150
Portland, OR 97232
971/673-0001, fax 971/673-0002
pharmacy.board@state.or.us
www.pharmacy.state.or.us

Pennsylvania

Melanie A. Zimmerman, Executive Secretary
PO Box 2649
Harrisburg, PA 17105-2649
717/783-7156, fax 717/787-7769
st-pharmacy@state.pa.us
www.dos.state.pa.us/pharm

Puerto Rico

Magda Bouet, Executive Director
Department of Health, Board of Pharmacy
Call Box 10200
Santurce, PR 00908
787/724-7282, fax 787/725-7903
mbouet@salud.gov.pr

Rhode Island

Catherine A. Cordy, Executive Director
3 Capitol Hill, Room 205
Providence, RI 02908-5097
401/222-2837, fax 401/222-2158
cathyc@doh.state.ri.us
www.health.ri.gov/hsr/professions/pharmacy.php

South Carolina

Lee Ann Bundrick, Administrator
Kingstree Bldg., 110 Centerview Dr., Suite 306
Columbia, SC 29210
803/896-4700, fax 803/896-4596
bundricl@llr.sc.gov
www.llronline.com/POL/pharmacy

South Dakota

Dennis M. Jones, Executive Secretary
4305 S. Louise Ave, Suite 104
Sioux Falls, SD 57106
605/362-2737, fax 605/362-2738
dennis.jones@state.sd.us
www.state.sd.us/doh/pharmacy

Tennessee

Terry Webb Grinder, Interim Executive Director
Tennessee Department of Commerce and Insurance
Board of Pharmacy
500 James Robertson Pkwy., 2nd Floor
Davy Crockett Tower, Nashville, TN 37243-1149
615/741-2718, fax 615/741-2722
terry.grinder@state.tn.us
www.state.tn.us/commerce/boards/pharmacy

Texas

Gay Dodson, Executive Director/Secretary
333 Guadalupe, Tower 3, Suite 600
Austin, TX 78701-3942
512/305-8000, fax 512/305-8082
gay.dodson@tsbp.state.tx.us
www.tsbp.state.tx.us

Utah

Diana L. Baker, Bureau Manager
PO Box 146741
Salt Lake City, UT 84114-6741
801/530-6179, fax 801/530-6511
dbaker@utah.gov
www.dopl.utah.gov

Vermont

Peggy Atkins, Board Administrator
Office of Professional Regulation
26 Terrace St.
Montpelier, VT 05609-1106
802/828-2373, fax 802/828-2465
patkins@sec.state.vt.us
www.vtprofessionals.org

Virgin Islands

Lydia T. Scott, Executive Assistant
Dept of Health, Schneider Regional Center
48 Sugar Estate
St. Thomas, VI 00802
340/774-0117, fax 340/777-4001
lydia.scott@usvi-doh.org

Virginia

Elizabeth Scott Russell, Executive Director
6603 W Broad St, 5th Floor
Richmond, VA 23230-1712
804/662-9911, fax 804/662-9313
scotti.russell@dhp.virginia.gov
www.dhp.state.va.us/pharmacy/default.htm

Washington

Lisa Salmi, Acting Executive Director
PO Box 47863
Olympia, WA 98504-7863
360/236-4825, fax 360/586-4359
Lisa.Salmi@doh.wa.gov
https://fortress.wa.gov/doh/hpqa1/HPS4/Pharmacy/default.htm

West Virginia

William T. Douglass, Jr, Executive Director and General Counsel
232 Capitol St.
Charleston, WV 25301
304/558-0558, fax 304/558-0572
wdouglass@wvbop.com
www.wvbop.com

Wisconsin

Tom Ryan, Bureau Director
1400 E. Washington, PO Box 8935
Madison, WI 53708-8935
608/266-2112, fax 608/267-0644
thomas.ryan@drl.state.wi.us
www.drl.state.wi.us

Wyoming

James T. Carder, Executive Director
632 S. David St., Casper, WY 82601
307/234-0294, fax 307/234-7226
wybop@state.wy.us
http://pharmacyboard.state.wy.us

Appendix Two

ADDRESSES AND WEB SITES OF PERTINENT PHARMACY ORGANIZATIONS

American Association of Pharmacy Technicians (AAPT)
PO Box 1447
Greensboro, NC 27402
877-368-4771/Fax: 336-333-9068
www.pharmacytechnician.com

American Society of Health-System Pharmacists (ASHP)
7272 Wisconsin Ave
Bethesda, MD 20814
www.ashp.org
Accredited training program site: www.ashp.org/directories/
    technicians/index.cfm

Canadian Association of Pharmacy Technicians (CAPT)
CAPT National
PO Box 1271, Station F
Toronto, ON, Canada M4Y2V8
www.capt.ca

National Pharmacy Technician Association (NAPT)
PO Box 683148
Houston, TX 77268-3148
888-247-8700/Fax: 888-247-8706
www.pharmacytechnician.org

Pharmacy Technician Certification Board (PTCB)
1100 15th St. NW, Suite 730
Washington, DC 20005-1707
800-363-8012/Fax: 202-429-7596
www.ptcb.org
Contains many links to state boards of pharmacy, state pharmaceutical
associations, and continuing education programs for technicians.

Pharmacy Technician Educators Council (PTEC)
Dolores Sewchok, President
1650 Metropolitan St., Suite 200
Pittsburgh, PA 15233
dsewchok@mcg-btc.org
www.rxptec.org

Pharmacy Technician Educators Council (PTEC)
Mary Mohr, PTEC President-Elect
6144 Knyghton Road
Indianapolis, IN 46220
mmohr@clarian.org

Appendix Three

LIST OF ACCREDITED PHARMACY TECHNICIAN PROGRAMS

Name of Site	Type	Code
Alabama		
George C. Wallace State Community College—Hanceville	Community College	AL-01
Alaska		
None		
Arizona		
Pima Community College	Community College	AZ-01
Arkansas		
None		
California		
American Career College	Technical College	CA-18
American Career College	Technical College	CA-27
American Career College	Vocational/Tech School	CA-33
Cerritos College	Community College	CA-17

Name of Site	Type	Code
Charles A. Jones Skills and Business Education Center	Technical College	CA-19
Charles R. Drew University of Medicine and Science	University	CA-24
Foothill College (Middlefield Campus)	Community College	CA-23
HealthStaff Training Institute	Vocational/Tech School	CA-05
HealthStaff Training Institute Branch	Vocational/Tech School	CA-29
North Orange County Community College District, School of Continuing Education	Community College	CA-30
North-West College	Vocational/Tech School	CA-04
North-West College	Vocational/Tech School	CA-11
North-West College	Vocational/Tech School	CA-10
North-West College	Vocational/Tech School	CA-12
Santa Ana College	Community College	CA-03
Western Career College—Antioch	Vocational/Tech School	CA-22
Western Career College—Citrus Heights	Technical/Community	CA-32
Western Career College—Emeryville	Vocational/Tech School	CA-28
Western Career College—Freemont	Vocational/Tech School	CA-21
Western Career College—Pleasant Hill	Vocational/Tech School	CA-26
Western Career College—Sacramento	Vocational/Tech School	CA-06
Western Career College—San Jose	Vocational/Tech School	CA-20
Western Career College—San Leandro	Vocational/Tech School	CA-13
Western Career College—Stockton	Vocational/Tech School	CA-31

Colorado

Arapahoe Community College	Community College	CO-02
Front Range Community College	Community College	CO-03

Connecticut

Briarwood College	Community College	CT-02

Delaware

None

District of Columbia

None

Name of Site	Type	Code
Florida		
Florida Metropolitan University—Melbourne Campus	University	FL-06
Henry W. Brewster Technical Center	Technical College	FL-02
Lake City Community College	Community College	FL-05
McFatter Vocational Technical Center	Vocational/Tech School	FL-03
Pinellas Technical Education Center	Vocational/Tech School	FL-01
Georgia		
Ogeechee Technical College	Technical College	GA-04
Southeastern Technical College	Technical College	GA-03
Southwest Georgia Technical College	Technical College	GA-02
Valdosta Technical College	Technical College	GA-01
Guam		
None		
Hawaii		
None		
Idaho		
None		
Illinois		
Blessing Hospital	Hospital	IL-04
Malcolm X College	Community College	IL-03
South Suburban College	Community College	IL-02
Walgreen Co.	Other	IL-05
Indiana		
Clarian Health Partners, Inc.	Hospital	IN-01
Iowa		
None		
Kansas		
None		

Name of Site	Type	Code
Kentucky		
St. Catharine College	Technical College	KY-01
Louisiana		
Bossier Parish Community College	Community College	LA-02
Delgado Community College	Community College	LA-04
Louisiana State University at Alexandria	Community College	LA-03
Maine		
None		
Maryland		
Anne Arundel Community College	Community College	MD-04
Massachusetts		
Holyoke Community College	Community College	MA-01
Michigan		
Henry Ford Community College	Community College	MI-02
Washtenaw Community College	Community College	MI-03
Wayne County Community College	Community College	MI-01
Minnesota		
Century Community and Technical College	Technical College	MN-01
Minnesota State Community and Technical College	Technical College	MN-03
Northland Community and Technical College	Technical College	MN-02
Mississippi		
Jones County Junior College	Community College	MS-02
Missouri		
St. Louis Community College at Forest Park	Community/Technical College	MO-01

Name of Site	Type	Code
Montana		
University of Montana–Missoula College of Technology	Technical College	MT-01
Nebraska		
None		
Nevada		
None		
New Hampshire		
None		
New Jersey		
None		
New Mexico		
None		
New York		
None		
North Carolina		
Durham Technical Community College	Community College	NC-01
North Dakota		
North Dakota State College of Science	Community/Technical College	ND-01
Ohio		
Collins Career Center	Vocational/Tech School	OH-03
Cuyahoga Community College	Community College	OH-01
Oklahoma		
None		
Oregon		
None		

Name of Site	Type	Code
Pennsylvania		
Bidwell Training Center, Inc.	Vocational/Tech School	PA-05
Community College of Allegheny County, South Campus	Community College	PA-03
Great Lakes Institute of Technology	Vocational/Tech School	PA-02
Western School of Health and Business Careers	Vocational/Tech School	PA-04
Puerto Rico		
None		
Rhode Island		
CVS/Pharmacy	Other	RI-01
South Carolina		
Greenville Technical College	Vocational/Tech School	SC-02
Horry-Georgetown Technical College	Technical College	SC-05
Midlands Technical College	Technical College	SC-01
Piedmont Technical College	Technical College	SC-06
Spartanburg Technical College	Technical College	SC-04
Trident Technical College	Community College	SC-03
South Dakota		
Western Dakota Technical Institute	Vocational/Tech School	SD-01
Tennessee		
Chattanooga State Technical Community College	Community College	TN-05
Concorde Career College	Technical College	TN-03
Tennessee Technology Center at Jackson	Vocational/Tech School	TN-07
Tennessee Technology Center at Memphis	Technical College	TN-06
Tennessee Technology Center at Murfreesboro	Vocational/Tech School	TN-04
Tennessee Technology Center at Nashville	Vocational/Tech School	TN-01
Walters State Community College	Community College	TN-08

Name of Site	Type	Code
Texas		
Amarillo College	Technical College	TX-22
Angelina College	Community College	TX-05
Austin Community College	Community College	TX-12
Cisco Junior College	Community College	TX-08
Coleman College of Health Sciences	Community College	TX-02
El Paso Community College	Community College	TX-06
Lamar State College—Orange	Community College	TX-10
National Institute of Technology	Vocational/Tech School	TX-21
North Harris College	Community College	TX-18
Northwest Vista College	Community College	TX-11
Richland College	Community College	TX-03
San Jacinto College, North	Community College	TX-14
San Jacinto College, South	Community College	TX-17
South Texas College	Technical/Community	TX-09
South Texas Vo-Tech	Vocational/Tech School	TX-15
The University of Texas Medical Branch	Hospital	TX-04
U.S. Army Medical Department Center and School	Military School	TX-01
United States Air Force School of Health Sciences	Military School	TX-07
Vernon College	Community/Technical College	TX-20
Weatherford College	Community College	TX-13
Utah		
None		
Vermont		
None		
Virgin Islands		
None		
Virginia		
Naval School of Health Sciences	Military School	VA-02

Name of Site	Type	Code
Washington		
Clover Park Technical College	Technical College	WA-04
Renton Technical College	Vocational/Tech School	WA-02
Spokane Community College	Community College	WA-03
St. Joseph Medical Center	Community College	WA-01
West Virginia		
Carver Career and Technical Education Center	Vocational/Tech School	WV-01
Wisconsin		
None		
Wyoming		
Casper College	Community/Technical College	WY-01

Appendix Four

LIST OF DRUG ENFORCEMENT ADMINISTRATION (DEA) FIELD OFFICES

DEA has 227 domestic offices throughout the United States and 86 foreign offices in 62 countries.

DOMESTIC OFFICES

Atlanta Division
(404) 893-7000
Offices
Augusta, GA
Columbus, GA
Macon, GA
Rome, GA
Savannah, GA
Ashville, NC
Charlotte, NC
Greensboro, NC
Raleigh, NC
Wilmington, NC
Beaufort, SC
Charleston, SC
Columbia, SC
Florence, SC
Greenville, SC
Chattanooga, TN
Jackson, TN
Johnson City, TN
Knoxville, TN
Memphis, TN
Nashville, TN

Boston Division
(617) 557-2100
Offices
Bridgeport, CT
Hartford, CT
New Haven, CT
New Bedford, MA
Springfield, MA
Bangor, ME
Portland, ME
Manchester, NH
Portsmouth, NH
Providence, RI
Burlington, VT

Caribbean Division
(787) 775-1815
Offices
Bridgetown,
 Barbados
Santo-Domingo,
 Dom. Rep.
Port-au-Prince, Haiti
Kingston, Jamaica
Curacao, Neth. Ant.
Ponce, Puerto Rico
Port of Spain, Trinidad
 and Tobago
St. Thomas, VI
St. Croix, VI

Chicago Division
(312) 353-7875
Offices
Rockford, IL
Springfield, IL
Evansville, IN
Ft. Wayne, IN
Indianapolis, IN
Merrillville, IN
Minneapolis/St. Paul,
 MN
Bismarck, ND
Fargo, ND
Green Bay, WI
Madison, WI
Milwaukee, WI

Dallas Division
(214) 366-6900
Offices
McAlester, OK
Oklahoma City, OK
Tulsa, OK
Amarillo, TX
Ft. Worth, TX
Lubbock, TX
Tyler, TX

Denver Division
(303) 705-7300
Offices
Colorado Springs,
 CO
Glenwood Springs,
 CO
Grand Junction, CO
Steamboat Springs,
 CO
Billings, MT
Missoula, MT
Salt Lake City, UT
St. George, UT
Casper, WY
Cheyenne, WY

Detroit Division
(313) 234-4000
Offices
Kalamazoo, MI
Lexington, KY
London, KY
Louisville, KY
Madisonville, KY
Lansing, MI
Grand Rapids, MI
Saginaw, MI
Cincinnati, OH
Cleveland, OH
Columbus, OH
Dayton, OH
Toledo, OH
Youngstown, OH

El Paso Division
(915) 832-6000
Offices
Albuquerque, NM
Las Cruces, NM
Alpine, TX
Midland, TX

Houston Division
(713) 693-3000
Offices
Austin, TX
Beaumont, TX
Brownsville, TX
Corpus Christi, TX
Del Rio, TX
Eagle Pass, TX
Galveston, TX
Laredo, TX
McAllen, TX
San Antonio, TX
Waco, TX

Los Angeles Division
(213) 621-6700
Offices
Riverside, CA
Santa Ana, CA
Ventura, CA
Guam
Hilo, HI
Honolulu, HI
Maui, HI
Lake Tahoe, NV
Las Vegas, NV
Reno, NV

Miami Division
(305) 994-4870
Offices
Freeport, Bahamas
Nassau, Bahamas
Ft. Lauderdale, FL
Ft. Myers, FL
Gainesville, FL
Jacksonville, FL
Key Largo, FL
Key West, FL
Orlando, FL
Panama City, FL
Pensacola, FL
Port St. Lucie, FL
Tallahassee, FL
Tampa, FL
Titusville, FL
W. Palm Beach, FL

New Jersey Division
(973) 776-1100
Offices
Atlantic City, NJ
Camden, NJ
Paterson, NJ

New Orleans Division
(504) 840-1100
Offices
Birmingham, AL
Huntsville, AL
Mobile, AL
Montgomery, AL
Fayetteville, AR
Ft. Smith, AR
Little Rock, AR
Baton Rouge, LA
Lafayette, LA
Monroe, LA
Shreveport, LA
Gulfport, MS
Jackson, MS
Oxford, MS

New York Division
(212) 337-3900
Offices
Albany, NY
Buffalo, NY
Long Island, NY
Plattsburgh, NY
Rochester, NY
Syracuse, NY
Westchester County, NY

Philadelphia Division
(215) 861-3474
Offices
Dover, DE
Wilmington, DE
Allentown, PA
Harrisburg, PA
Pittsburgh, PA
Scranton, PA

Phoenix Division
(602) 664-5600
Offices
Flagstaff, AZ
Lake Havasu City, AZ
Nogales, AZ
Sierra Vista, AZ
Tucson, AZ
Yuma, AZ

San Diego Division
(858) 616-4100
Offices
Carlsbad, CA
Imperial County, CA
San Ysidro, CA

San Francisco Division
(415) 436-7900
Offices
Bakersfield, CA
Fresno, CA
Modesto, CA
Oakland, CA
Redding, CA
Sacramento, CA
San Jose, CA
Santa Rosa, CA

Seattle Division
(206) 553-5443
Offices
Anchorage, AK
Fairbanks, AK
Boise, ID
Bend, OR
Eugene, OR
Medford, OR
Portland, OR
Salem, OR
Blaine, WA
Spokane, WA
Tacoma, WA
Tri-Cities, WA
Yakima, WA

St. Louis Division
(314) 538-4600
Offices
Cedar Rapids, IA
Des Moines, IA
Sioux City, IA
Carbondale, IL
Fairview Heights, IL
Quad Cities, IL
Garden City, KS
Kansas City, KS
Topeka, KS
Wichita, KS
Cape Giradeau, MO
Jefferson City, MO
Springfield, MO
North Platte, NE
Omaha, NE
Rapid City, SD
Sioux Falls, SD

Washington, DC Division
(202) 305-8500
Offices
Baltimore, MD
Hagerstown, MD
Salisbury, MD
Bristol, VA
Hampton, VA
Norfolk, VA
Richmond, VA
Roanoke, VA
Winchester, VA
Charleston, WV
Clarksburg, WV
Wheeling, WV

FOREIGN OFFICES

South America
Asuncion, Paraguay
Bogota, Colombia
Cartagena, Colombia
Brasilia, Brazil
Sao Paulo, Brazil
Buenos Aires,
 Argentina
Caracas, Venezuela
La Paz, Bolivia
Cochabamba, Bolivia
Santa Cruz, Bolivia
Trinidad, Bolivia
Lima, Peru
Quito, Ecuador
Guayaquil, Ecuador
Santiago, Chile

Mexico/Central America
Belize City, Belize
Guatemala City,
 Guatemala
Managua, Nicaragua
Mexico City, Mexico
Ciudad Juarez, Mexico
Guadalajara, Mexico
Hermosillo, Mexico
Mazatlan, Mexico
Merida, Mexico
Monterrey, Mexico
Tijuana, Mexico
Panama City, Panama
San Jose, Costa Rica
San Salvador, El
 Salvador
Tegucigalpa, Honduras

Caribbean
Bridgetown, Barbados
Curacao, Netherlands
 Antilles
Kingston, Jamaica
Port of Spain, Trinidad
 and Tobago
Port-au-Prince, Haiti
Santo Domingo, Dom.
 Rep.
Nassau, Bahamas
Freeport, Bahamas

Europe/Mideast/Africa
Ankara, Turkey
Istanbul, Turkey
Athens, Greece
Bern, Switzerland
Berlin, Germany
Frankfurt, Germany
Brussels, Belgium
Cairo, Egypt
Copenhagen, Denmark
Islamabad, Pakistan
Peshawar, Pakistan
Kabul, Afghanistan
Lagos, Nigeria
London, England

Madrid, Spain
Moscow, Russia
New Delhi, India
Nicosia, Cyprus
Ottawa, Canada
Vancouver, Canada
Paris, France
Pretoria, South Africa
Rome, Italy
Milan, Italy
Tashkent, Uzbekistan
The Hague, Netherlands
Vienna, Austria

Far East
Bangkok, Thailand
Chiang Mai, Thailand
Udorn, Thailand
Beijing, China
Canberra, Australia
Hanoi, Vietnam
Hong Kong, China
Kuala Lumpur,
  Malaysia
Manila, Philippines
Rangoon, Burma
Seoul, Korea
Singapore, Singapore
Tokyo, Japan
Vientiane, Laos

Appendix Five

SAMPLE DEA FORMS

NEW NAME
Butler Animal Health Supply, LLC

⁓⁓**SAMPLE DEA FORM 222** ⁓⁓

Place this sample with your blank DEA Form 222s for quick reference. Use this sample and the
"7-Step Checklist" (below) to ensure your form is correct before mailing.

See Reverse of PURCHASER'S Copy for Instructions	No order form may be issued for Schedules I and II substances unless a completed application form has been received (21 CFR 1305.04).	OMB APPROVAL No. 1117-0010

TO: *(Name of Supplier)* **Butler AHS, LLC** *or* **Butler Animal Health Supply, LLC** **(1*)**		STREET ADDRESS **3820 Twin Creeks Drive**
CITY and STATE COLUMBUS, OH 43204	DATE **(2*)**	TO BE FILLED IN BY SUPPLIER SUPPLIER'S DEA REGISTRATION NO.

L I N E No.	No. of Package	Size of Package	Name of Item	National Drug Code									Packages Shipped	Date Shipped
			TO BE FILLED IN BY PURCHASER											
1	**(3*)**	250 ML	Socumb, 6 Grain											
2		20 ML	Hydromorphone Inj 2 MG											
3		5x10ml	Morphine Sulfate 1MG											
etc.		100	Morphine Tabs, 30 MG											
.		20 ML	Morphine Sulfate, 15 MG											
.		25 X 50 ML	Fentanyl CIT, 0.05 MG											
.		20 ML	Demerol HCL, 100 MG											
.		30 ML	Demerol HCL, 50 MG											
.		100	Demerol Tabs, 50 MG											
.		5	Fentanyl Patches *(see below)											
.		100ml	Sleepaway, 260 mg											

▲ **(4*)** LAST LINE COMPLETED *(MUST BE 10 OR LESS)*	SIGNATURE OF PURCHASER OR HIS ATTORNEY OR AGENT	**(5*)**
Date Issued	DEA Registration No.	(Name and Address of Registrant) (NOTE: THE NAME AND ADDRESS APPEARING IN THIS BLOCK MUST BE EXACTLY THE SAME AS THE NAME AND ADDRESS ON THE DEA FORM 223 - CONTROLLED SUBSTANCE REGISTRATION)
Schedules		
Registered as a	Form No.	

U.S. OFFICIAL ORDER FORMS - SCHEDULES I & II
SUPPLIER'S COPY 1
* Indicate Fentanyl Patches as 25mcg, 50mcg, 75mcg, or 100mcg

---

"7-Step Checklist"

1. Name of supplier, address, city and state are correct.
2. Form is dated.
3. Number of packages, size of package, and strength desired is correct.
4. The "NO. OF LINES COMPLETED" block is filled in.
5. Veterinarian has signed the form.
6. Form contains no erasures or alterations.
7. Remove the purchaser's copy (blue copy) and place in your records.

Revised 7/8/2005

U.S. Department of Justice
Drug Enforcement Administration

REPORT OF THEFT OR LOSS OF CONTROLLED SUBSTANCES

Federal Regulations require registrants to submit a detailed report of any theft or loss of Controlled Substances to the Drug Enforcement Administration.

Complete the front and back of this form in triplicate. Forward the original and duplicate copies to the nearest DEA Office. Retain the triplicate copy for your records. Some states may also require a copy of this report.

OMB APPROVAL
No. 1117-0001

1. Name and Address of Registrant (include ZIP Code) ZIP CODE	2. Phone No. (Include Area Code)

3. DEA Registration Number 2 ltr. prefix 7 digit suffix	4. Date of Theft or Loss	5. Principal Business of Registrant (Check one)

5. Principal Business of Registrant (Check one)
1 ☐ Pharmacy   5 ☐ Distributor
2 ☐ Practitioner   6 ☐ Methadone Program
3 ☐ Manufacturer   7 ☐ Other (Specify)
4 ☐ Hospital/Clinic

6. County in which Registrant is located	7. Was Theft reported to Police? ☐ Yes ☐ No	8. Name and Telephone Number of Police Department (Include Area Code)

9. Number of Thefts or Losses Registrant has experienced in the past 24 months	10. Type of Theft or Loss (Check one and complete items below as appropriate)

10. Type of Theft or Loss (Check one and complete items below as appropriate)
1 ☐ Night break-in   3 ☐ Employee pilferage   5 ☐ Other (Explain)
2 ☐ Armed robbery   4 ☐ Customer theft   6 ☐ Lost in transit (Complete Item 14)

11. If Armed Robbery, was anyone: Killed? ☐ No ☐ Yes (How many) _____ Injured? ☐ No ☐ Yes (How many) _____	12. Purchase value to registrant of Controlled Substances taken? $	13. Were any pharmaceuticals or merchandise taken? ☐ No ☐ Yes (Est. Value) $

14. IF LOST IN TRANSIT, COMPLETE THE FOLLOWING:

A. Name of Common Carrier	B. Name of Consignee	C. Consignee's DEA Registration Number

D. Was the carton received by the customer? ☐ Yes ☐ No	E. If received, did it appear to be tampered with? ☐ Yes ☐ No	F. Have you experienced losses in transit from this same carrier in the past? ☐ No ☐ Yes (How Many) _____

15. What identifying marks, symbols, or price codes were on the labels of these containers that would assist in identifying the products?

16. If Official Controlled Substance Order Forms (DEA-222) were stolen, give numbers.

17. What security measures have been taken to prevent future thefts or losses?

FORM DEA - 106 (11-00) *Previous editions obsolete*   **CONTINUE ON REVERSE**

COPY

FORM DEA-106 (Nov. 2000) Pg. 2

LIST OF CONTROLLED SUBSTANCES LOST

Trade Name of Substance or Preparation	Name of Controlled Substance in Preparation	Dosage Strength and Form	Quantity
Examples: Desoxyn	Methamphetamine Hydrochloride	5 mg Tablets	3 x 100
Demerol	Meperidine Hydrochloride	50 mg/ml Vial	5 x 30 ml
Robitussin A-C	Codeine Phosphate	2 mg/cc Liquid	12 Pints
1.			
2.			
3.			
4.			
5.			
6.			
7.			
8.			
9.			
10.			
11.			
12.			
13.			
14.			
15.			
16.			
17.			
18.			
19.			
20.			
21.			
22.			
23.			
24.			
25.			
26.			
27.			
28.			
29.			
30.			
31.			
32.			
33.			
34.			
35.			
36.			
37.			
38.			
39.			
40.			
41.			
42.			
43.			
44.			
45.			
46.			
47.			
48.			
49.			
50.			

I certify that the foregoing information is correct to the best of my knowledge and belief.

Signature   Title   Date

COPY

Appendix Six

LEGAL STANDING OF PHARMACY TECHNICIANS

Status of Pharmacy Technicians

State	Designation	Does State: License Technicians?	Register Technicians?	Certify Technicians?	Technician Registration Fee	Registration Renewal Schedule
Alabama	Pharmacy Technician	No	Yes	No	$20/year	Biennial
Alaska	Pharmacy Technician	Yes	No	No	$25 HH	Biennial
Arizona	Pharmacy Technician	Yes	No	No	B	Biennial
Arkansas	Pharmacy Technician	No	Yes	No	$70	Biennial
California	Pharmacy Technician	Yes	Yes	No	$50	Biennial
Colorado	Unlicensed Personnel, Unlicensed Assistant	No	No	No	N/A	N/A
Connecticut	Pharmacy Technician	No	Yes	No	$50	Annual, 3/31
Delaware	Supportive Personnel	No	No	No	None	N/A
District of Columbia	Ancillary Personnel	No	No	No	—	—
Florida	Pharmacy Technician	No	No	No	N/A	N/A
Georgia	Ancillary Personnel	No	No	No	—	—
Guam	Pharmacy Technician	No	Yes	No	R, J	R, J
Hawaii	Pharmacy Technician	No	No	No	N/A	N/A
Idaho	Pharmacy Technician	No	Yes	No	$35	Annual
Illinois	Pharmacy Technician	No	Yes	No	$40 initial; $25 renewal	Annual
Indiana	Pharmacy Technician	No	No	Yes	$25	Biennial
Iowa	Pharmacy Technician	No	Yes	No	$44	Z

State	Title				Fee	Renewal
Kansas	Pharmacy Technician	No	Yes	No	$25	Biennial
Kentucky	Pharmacy Technician	No J	No J	No J	N/A	N/A
Louisiana	Pharmacy Technician	No	No	Yes	$100	Annual
Maine	Pharmacy Technician	No	Yes	No	$20	Annual
Maryland	Unlicensed Person	No	No	No	N/A	N/A
Massachusetts	Pharmacy Technician	No	Yes	No	$51	Biennial G
Michigan	Pharmacy Personnel	No	No	No	—	—
Minnesota	Pharmacy Technician	No	Yes	No	$20	Annual
Mississippi	Pharmacy Technician L	No	Yes Q	No	$25	Annual
Missouri	Pharmacy Technician	No	Yes	No	$10 W	Annual
Montana	Pharmacy Technician	No	Yes	Yes AA	$40 initial; $25 renewal	Annual
Nebraska	Pharmacy Technician	No	No	No	—	—
Nevada	Pharmaceutical Technician L	No	Yes	No	$40	Biennial
New Hampshire	Pharmacy Technician	No	Yes	No	$25	Annual, 4/01
New Jersey	Pharmacy Technician	No	Yes	No	N/A	N/A
New Mexico	Pharmacy Technician N	No	Yes	No	$30	Biennial
New York	Unlicensed Person	No	No	No	N/A	N/A
North Carolina	Pharmacy Technician	No	Yes	No	$25	Annual
North Dakota	Registered Pharmacy Technician	No	Yes	No	$35	Annual
Ohio	F	No	No	No	N/A	N/A
Oklahoma	Pharmacy Technician	No	Yes O	No	$40	GG
Oregon	Pharmacy Technician	No	Yes	No	$35	1 year, Sept.
Pennsylvania	Pharmacy Technician	No	No	No	N/A	N/A

Status of Pharmacy Technicians (Continued)

| State | Designation | Does State: | | | Technician Registration Fee | Registration Renewal Schedule |
		License Technicians?	Register Technicians?	Certify Technicians?		
Puerto Rico	Pharmacy Assistant	No	Yes	Yes	—	—
Rhode Island	Pharmacy Technician	Yes	No	No	$25	Annual
South Carolina	Pharmacy Technician	No	Yes	Yes	$40 initial; $25 renewal	Annual
South Dakota	Pharmacy Technician	No	Yes	No	$25	Annual
Tennessee	Pharmacy Technician	No	Yes	No	$50-biennial	Cyclical
Texas	Pharmacy Technician	No	Yes	No	$56 initial; $53 renewal	Biennial
Utah	Pharmacy Technician	Yes	No	No	$60	Biennial
Vermont	Pharmacy Technician	No	Yes	No	$25	Biennial
Virginia	Pharmacy Technician	No	Yes A	No	$25	Annual
Washington	Pharmacy Technician	No	No	Yes	$50	Annual
West Virginia	Pharmacy Technician	No	Yes	No	$25 X	Biennial
Wisconsin	Pharmacy Technician	No	No	No	—	—
Wyoming	Registered Pharmacy Technician K	Yes*	Yes*	No	$35	Annual

* See Footnotes (*) on page 146.

Status of Pharmacy Technicians (Continued)

State	Technician Training Requirements	Technician CE Requirements	Technician Examination Requirement	Can Board Deny, Revoke, Suspend, or Restrict Technician Registration?	Maximum Ratio of Technician(s) to Pharmacist in an: Ambulatory Care Setting	Institutional Care Setting
Alabama	No	3 h/yr H	—	Yes	3:1*	3:1*
Alaska	Yes S	10 h/2 yr	No	Yes	None	None
Arizona	Yes	PTCB	Yes PTCB	Yes	None	None
Arkansas	No	None	No	Yes	2:1	2:1
California	Yes	No	No CC	Yes	Varies*	2:1
Colorado	No	N/A	No	N/A	2:1	2:1
Connecticut	Yes S	No	No	Yes	2:1* or 3:1	3:1*
Delaware	Yes	N/A	No	N/A	None	None
District of Columbia	No	—	—	—	—	—
Florida	No	None	No	N/A	3:1	3:1
Georgia	No	None	No	N/A	3:1*	3:1*
Guam	No R, J	None R, J	No	Yes	None R, J	None R, J
Hawaii	No	N/A	No	No	None	None
Idaho	Yes	No	No	No	3:1	3:1
Illinois	No J	No		Yes	None	None
Indiana	Yes	N/A	No U	Yes	4:1*	4:1*
Iowa	Yes*	No	No	Yes	None	None
Kansas	Yes	No	Yes	Yes	2:1	2:1

Status of Pharmacy Technicians (Continued)

State	Technician Training Requirements	Technician CE Requirements	Technician Examination Requirement	Can Board Deny, Revoke, Suspend, or Restrict Technician Registration?	Maximum Ratio of Technician(s) to Pharmacist in an: Ambulatory Care Setting	Institutional Care Setting
Kentucky	No	None	No	N/A	None	None
Louisiana	Yes	10 h	Yes	Yes	2:1	2:1
Maine	Yes	No	No	Yes	3:1*	3:1*
Maryland	No	N/A	No	N/A	—	—
Massachusetts	Yes	No BB	Yes	Yes	4:1*	4:1*
Michigan	No	—	—	—	None	None
Minnesota	No	No	No	Yes	2:1*	2:1*
Mississippi	No I	No	No	Yes	2:1	2:1
Missouri	No	None	No	Yes	None	None
Montana	Yes** T	Yes PTCB	Yes AA	Yes	1:1*	1:1*
Nebraska	Yes** I	—	—	—	2:1	2:1
Nevada	Yes	No Y	No	Yes	2:1	2:1
New Hampshire	No	None	No	Yes	None	None
New Jersey	No	No	—	Yes	Varies	Varies
New Mexico	Yes**	None	Yes AA	Yes	4:1	4:1
New York	No	No	No	No	2:1	2:1
North Carolina	Yes	None	No	Yes	2:1*	2:1*
North Dakota	Yes*	Yes, 20 h/2 yr	No FF	Yes	3:1	4:1

Ohio	No	No	No	No	None	None
Oklahoma	Yes	None	No	Yes	2:1	2:1
Oregon	Yes	No	No	Yes P	None	None
Pennsylvania	No	None	No	N/A	—	—
Puerto Rico	Yes*				None	None
Rhode Island	Yes	None	—	Yes	None	None
South Carolina	Yes DD	10 h/yr EE	Yes DD	Yes	3:1*	Varies*
South Dakota	No	None	No	Yes	2:1	2:1
Tennessee	No	None	No	Yes	2:1*	2:1*
Texas	Yes C	D	Yes	Yes	2:1*	None
Utah	Yes	20 h/2 yr	Yes E	Yes	3:1	3:1
Vermont	No	No	No	Yes	None	None
Virginia	Yes V	5 h/yr	Yes A, V	Yes	4:1	4:1
Washington	Yes	None	No	Yes	3:1 M	3:1 M
West Virginia	Yes I	None	Yes	Yes	4:1	4:1
Wisconsin	No	—	—	—	4:1	4:1
Wyoming	Yes I	6 h	Yes AA	Yes	3:1	3:1

PTCB, Pharmacy Technician Certification Board.
* See Footnotes (*) on page 146.
**Contact the state board of pharmacy office to obtain requirements.

Legend

A — As of February 26, 2004, have to be registered with board.
B — Technician trainee, $35; certified technician – $50.
C — A person may be a technician trainee for no more than 1 year while seeking certification through Pharmacy Technician Certification Board (PTCB). Contact the board for specific on-site training requirements.

Status of Pharmacy Technicians (Continued)

D — Same as PTCB requirements.

E — PTCB examination and Utah law examination.

F — The use of pharmacy technicians is not addressed in state statutes or regulations.

G — Biennial at birthday.

H — Effective January 1, 2002.

I — Training requirements developed by training pharmacies and approved by the board.

J — The board is proposing/developing regulations.

K — Designated as a "technician-in-training" prior to meeting requirements for licensure.

L — The term "support personnel" is also used.

M — A pharmacy may use more technicians than the prescribed 3:1 on approval of the board.

N — A "pharmacy technician" is a subset of "supportive personnel."

O — Technicians are not considered "registered" but are issued a "permit."

P — Cannot revoke, suspend, or restrict a technician registration but can deny an initial or renewal registration.

Q — As of January 1, 1999.

R — Not yet established.

S — On-the-job training by pharmacist-in-charge (PIC) appropriate to technician's duties.

T — Technician utilization plan filed with board or didactic course.

U — However, passage of the PTCB examination is one way to become certified as a technician in this state.

V — To be eligible for registration, a pharmacy technician must either hold current PTCB certification or must have passed a training program and examination approved by the board.

W — Plus a $38 fingerprint fee.

X — $25 initial; $30 renewal/2 years.

Y — However, technicians must complete 6 hours of in-service training per year.

Z — Biennial by birth month.

AA — PTCB certification required.

BB — However, "certified pharmacy technicians" must maintain certification.

CC — PTCB examination is one way to qualify for technician registration.

DD — An individual may be certified by the board as a pharmacy technician if the individual has worked for 1500 hours under the supervision of a licensed pharmacist as a registered pharmacy technician or has completed a Board of Pharmacy-approved pharmacy technician course as provided for in Subsection (D); however, beginning July 1, 2004, to be certified as a pharmacy technician an individual must have worked for 1000 hours under the supervision of a licensed pharmacist as a technician and must have completed a Board of Pharmacy-approved technician course as provided for in Subsection (D); a high school diploma or equivalent; and passed the National Pharmacy Technician Certification Examination or a Board of Pharmacy-approved examination and maintained current certification; and fulfilled continuing education (CE) requirements as provided for in Section 40-43-130(G). Contact the State Board of Pharmacy for further information.

EE — As a condition of registration renewal, a registered pharmacy technician shall complete 10 hours of Accreditation Council for Pharmacy Education- or Continuing Medical Education I-approved CE each year, beginning with the next renewal period after June 30, 2003. A minimum of 4 hours of the total hours must be obtained through attendance at lectures, seminars, or workshops.

FF — Requires PTCB examination for reciprocity.

GG — Annual (by birth month).

HH — Plus one-time application fee of $50.

NABPLAW Online Search Terms (*type as indicated below*)
Status of Pharmacy Technicians

- technician & requirements
- support & personnel & requirements
- technician & training
- technician & registration

Note: "ancillary personnel," "support personnel," and "nonlicensed personnel" can be substituted for "technician."

Status of Pharmacy Technicians (Continued)

Footnotes*

AL — 3:1 if one technician is PTCB certified. All techs must be at least 17.

CA — In community pharmacy, the ratio is 1:1 for the first pharmacist on duty, then 2:1 for each additional pharmacist on duty. 2:1 if pharmacy services patients of skilled nursing facilities or hospices. A pharmacist may also supervise one pharmacy technician trainee gaining required practical experience. In addition to a pharmacy technician, a nonlicensed person may type a prescription label, enter data into a computer record system, and obtain a prescription refill authorization.

CT — Refer to Section 20-576-36 of the Regulations of CT State Agencies. In summary, ratio not to exceed 2:1 when both technicians are registered. Ratio of 3:1 permitted when there are two registered technicians and one certified technician. However, a pharmacist is permitted to refuse the 3:1 ratio for the 2:1 ratio. In an institutional outpatient pharmacy, ratio is 2:1. The pharmacist manager may petition the commission to increase ratio to 3:1 in a licensed or institutional outpatient pharmacy. Inpatient pharmacy ratio is 3:1 generally, but pharmacy can petition for ratio of up to 5:1; satellite pharmacy 3:1, but can petition for up to 5:1.

GA — Board may consider and approve an application to increase the ratio in a hospital pharmacy.

IA — Technicians must be under the immediate and personal supervision of the pharmacist. Technician training must be documented and maintained.

IN — Technicians must be under the immediate and personal supervision of the pharmacist.

MA — 3:1 provided one intern and one certified technician. 4:1 provided at least two certified technicians or one certified technician and one intern.

ME — 4:1 with an advanced pharmacy technician.

MN — Specific functions are exempted from the 2:1 ratio as follows: for intravenous admixture preparation, unit dose dispensing, prepackaging, and bulk compounding, ratio is 3:1. One additional technician per pharmacy if that technician is PTCB certified.

MT — Ratio is 2:1 if both are performing the following procedures: intravenous admixture or sterile product preparation; filling of unit dose cassettes; prepackaging; or bulk compounding. Licensee may ask board for variance based on established criteria or greater on board approval.

NC — Ratio may be increased above 2:1 if additional technicians are certified.

ND — Technicians must complete American Society of Health-System Pharmacists®—accredited approved academic program or on-the-job training program.

PR — 3000 hours of internship under direct supervision of a registered pharmacist and passing an examination prepared by the board are required for certification. 2000 hours may be substituted by completion of a vocational or technical pharmacy assistant accredited course. Designated "pharmacy assistant apprentice" until certified.

SC — The PIC shall develop and implement written policies and procedures to specify the duties to be performed by pharmacy technicians. The duties and responsibilities of these personnel shall be consistent with their training and experience. These policies and procedures shall, at a minimum, specify that pharmacy technicians are to be personally supervised by a licensed pharmacist who has the ability to control and who is responsible for the activities of pharmacy technicians, and that pharmacy technicians are not assigned duties that may be performed only by a licensed pharmacist. One pharmacist may not supervise more than three pharmacy technicians at a time; through June 30, 2006, at least one of these three technicians must be state certified, and after June 30, 2006, at least two of these three technicians must be state certified. If a pharmacist supervises only one or two pharmacy technicians, then these technicians are not required to be state certified. Pharmacy technicians do not include personnel in the prescription area performing only clerical functions, including data entry up to the point of dispensing, as defined in Section 40-43-30(14).

TN — 3:1 if technician is certified.

TX — 3:1 if at least one of the technicians is registered. Only one of the technicians may be involved in the compounding of sterile pharmaceuticals.

WY — "Technicians-in-training" are registered until they meet the requirements for licensure. The technician-in-training permit is valid for no more than 2 years from date of issue.

Pharmacy Technicians in Hospital/Institutional Setting

State	May Pharmacy Technicians in the Hospital/Institutional Setting:					
	Accept Called-In Rx from Physician's Office?	Enter Prescription into Computer?	Check the Work of Other Technicians?	Call Physician for Refill Authorization?	Compound Medications for Dispensing?	Transfer Prescriptions via Telephone?
Alabama	No	Yes	No	Yes D	No	No
Alaska G	No	Yes	No	Yes D	Yes	No
Arizona	No	Yes B	No	Yes B	Yes B	No
Arkansas	No	Yes	No	Yes D	Yes	No
California	No	Yes	No BB	Yes	Yes	No
Colorado	No	Yes	Yes	Yes D	Yes	No
Connecticut	No K	Yes	No	Yes D	Yes E	No
Delaware	No	Yes E	No	No	Yes F	No
District of Columbia	Yes V	Yes V	No	Yes V	Yes V	No
Florida	No	Yes	No	Yes	Yes	No
Georgia	No	Yes	No	No	No W	No
Guam	No	Yes E, G	No	No	Yes E, G	Pending regulations
Hawaii	No	Yes E, G	No	No	Yes E, G	No
Idaho	No	Yes	No	Yes	Yes	No
Illinois	H	Yes E	No	Yes E	Yes E	—
Indiana	No J	Yes	No	Yes	Yes	No
Iowa G	Yes	Yes	No	Yes	Yes	No

Kansas	No	Yes G	P	Yes	Yes G	No
Kentucky	No K	Yes E	Yes	Yes E, D	Yes E	No
Louisiana	No	Yes	No	Yes D	Yes E	No
Maine GG	No	Yes	No	Yes	Yes	No
Maryland	No	Yes G	No	Yes X	Yes G	No
Massachusetts	Yes AA	Yes G	Yes G	Yes	Yes B, G	No
Michigan	Yes G	Yes G	Yes C	No	Yes G	Yes Q
Minnesota	No	Yes	No	Yes	No	No
Mississippi E, G	No	Yes	No	Yes	Yes	No
Missouri	Yes E, G	Yes E, G	No	Yes E, G	Yes E, G	Yes E, G, CC
Montana DD	Z	Yes I	No Y	Yes D	Yes	No
Nebraska	No	Yes	No	Yes	Yes	No
Nevada	No	Yes	No	Yes	Yes	No
New Hampshire	No	Yes G	No	No	Yes G	No
New Jersey	No	Yes G	No	Yes D	Yes E, G	No
New Mexico	No	Yes	No	Yes G	Yes	No
New York	No	Yes G	No	No	No	No
North Carolina	Yes FF	Yes	No	Yes FF	Yes E	Yes FF
North Dakota	Yes	Yes	Yes G	Yes	Yes G	Yes
Ohio	No	Yes G	No	No	Yes E	No
Oklahoma	No	Yes	No	Yes D	Yes L	No
Oregon	No	Yes	No	Yes D	Yes	No
Pennsylvania E, G	No	Yes	No	No	Yes F	No
Puerto Rico	N	N	—	N	N	—
Rhode Island	No J, V	Yes	No	Yes	Yes G	No
South Carolina	Yes AA	Yes E	Yes M	Yes M	Yes E	Yes M

Pharmacy Technicians in Hospital/Institutional Setting (Continued)

| State | May Pharmacy Technicians in the Hospital/Institutional Setting: | | | | | |
	Accept Called-In Rx from Physician's Office?	Enter Prescription into Computer?	Check the Work of Other Technicians?	Call Physician for Refill Authorization?	Compound Medications for Dispensing?	Transfer Prescriptions via Telephone?
South Dakota	No	No O	No	No	Yes G	No
Tennessee	Yes U	Yes G	No S	Yes G	Yes G	Yes U
Texas	No	Yes	No	Yes D	Yes E, R	No
Utah	No	Yes G, I	No	Yes D	Yes G	Yes G, D
Vermont	No	Yes E	No	No	Yes A, B	No
Virginia	No	Yes G	No	Yes D	Yes E, G	No
Washington	No	Yes	Yes EE	Yes D	Yes T	No
West Virginia	No	Yes G	No	Yes D	Yes T	No
Wisconsin	Z	Yes	No	Z, D	Yes B, G	No
Wyoming E, G	No	Yes	—	Yes D	Yes G	No

Legend

A — Activities not addressed in statutes or regulations.

B — Subject to approved policy and procedure manuals, supportive personnel training, and pharmacist final verification and initialing.

C — Yes only after obtaining a variance from the board.

D — If there are any changes to the prescription and/or if professional consultation is involved, then the pharmacist must handle the call.

E — Allowed activity must be under the direct supervision of a licensed pharmacist. (HI, "immediate supervision." KY, Direct supervision if technician is not certified by the Pharmacy Technician Certification Board; if certified, then technician may perform activity under indirect supervision. LA, "Direct and immediate" supervision.)

F — Compounding is the responsibility of the pharmacist or pharmacy intern under the direct supervision of the pharmacist. The pharmacist may utilize the assistance of supportive personnel under certain conditions. Contact board for requirements.

G — Pharmacist must verify, check, and/or is responsible for allowed activities.

H — Not prohibited. Law and regulations are silent on this issue; however, the practice is discouraged. Pharmacists should exercise professional judgment.

I — Allowed activity must be under the general supervision of a licensed pharmacist.

J — Unless it is regarding a refill.

K — Allowed activity limited to pharmacist interns.

L — Bulk compounding allowed.

M — A supervising pharmacist may authorize a certified pharmacy technician to (1) receive and initiate verbal telephone orders; (2) conduct one-time prescription transfers; (3) check a technician's refill of medications if the medication is to be administered by a licensed health care professional in an institutional setting; and (4) check a technician's repackaging of medications from bulk to unit dose in an institutional setting.

N — Pharmacy Act allows pharmacy assistants to perform the tasks assigned by the pharmacist under his/her direct supervision. PR Supreme Court has recognized that only pharmacists are prepared to do patient counseling.

O — May key-in but not enter.

P — Need board approval.

Q — Yes, if there are policies and procedures in place that allow delegation and that comply with Board Administrative Rules 338.490 and 338.3162. Contact the State Board of Pharmacy for further information.

R — Must have special training. Contact the board for training requirements.

S — Under review/possible revision.

T — Bulk compounding and intravenous preparation are allowed, but "extemporaneous" compounding is not allowed.

U — If technician is certified.

Pharmacy Technicians in Hospital/Institutional Setting (Continued)

V — Pharmacist must verify, check, and/or is responsible for allowed activities; except in the case of Schedule II controlled substances, only a pharmacist may receive an oral prescription.

W — May compound intravenous admixtures only if pharmacist verifies the final product for accuracy, efficacy, patient utilization and has a mechanism to verify the measuring of active ingredients added to the intravenous mixture.

X — Pharmacy technician may call for refills for prescriptions other than controlled dangerous substances. May not accept refill authorization that changes the order.

Y — Pilot programs are under way.

Z — Can accept refills if no changes. (WI, new prescriptions must be recorded.)

AA — Certified technicians only with supervising pharmacist authorization. (MA, dependent on Department of Public Health approval.)

BB — However, CA has approved a study on this issue.

CC — May not transfer controlled substance prescriptions.

DD — Technicians can now work up to 30 minutes alone in the pharmacy while a pharmacist has a mandatory lunch break (up to 30 minutes) on the premises.

EE — Hospitals may apply to the board for approval of technician-check-technician programs that meet certain conditions. This is available for unit dose drug distribution systems.

FF — Board-certified technicians only.

GG — May accept called-in prescription from physician office only if an advanced technician.

**NABPLAW Online Search Terms *(type as indicated below)*
Pharmacy Technicians in Hospital/Institutional Setting**

- technician & requirements & hospital
- support & personnel & requirements & hospital
- technician & training & hospital
- technician & registration & hospital

Note: "ancillary personnel," "support personnel," and "nonlicensed personnel" can be substituted for "technician"; "institutional" can be substituted for "hospital."

Pharmacy Technicians in Community Setting

State	May Pharmacy Technicians in the Community Setting:					
	Accept Called-In Rx from Physician's Office?	Enter Prescription into Computer?	Check the Work of Other Technicians?	Call Physician for Refill Authorization?	Compound Medications for Dispensing?	Transfer Prescriptions via Telephone?
Alabama	No	Yes	No	Yes M	No	No
Alaska E	No	Yes	No	Yes M	Yes	No
Arizona	No	Yes B	No	Yes B	Yes R	No
Arkansas	No	Yes	No	Yes M	Yes D, E	No
California	No	Yes	No	Yes D	Yes D, E	No
Colorado	No	Yes	Yes	Yes	Yes E	No
Connecticut	No	Yes D, E	No	Yes M	Yes D, E	No
Delaware	No	Yes D	No	No	Yes F	No
District of Columbia	Yes S	Yes S	No	Yes S	Yes S	No
Florida	No	Yes	No	Yes	Yes	No
Georgia	No	Yes	No	No	No	No
Guam	No	Yes D, E	No	No	Yes D, E	Pending regulations
Hawaii	No	Yes D, E	No	No	Yes D, E	No
Idaho	No	Yes	No	Yes	Yes	No
Illinois	Q	Yes I	—	Yes I	Yes I	No
Indiana	No G	Yes	No	Yes	Yes	No
Iowa E	Yes	Yes	No	Yes	Yes	No
Kansas	No	Yes E	No	Yes	Yes E	No

State						
Kentucky	No H	Yes D	No	Yes D, M	Yes D	No
Louisiana	No	Yes	No	Yes M	Yes D	No
Maine BB	No	Yes	No	Yes	Yes	No
Maryland	No	Yes E	No	Yes W	Yes E	No
Massachusetts	Yes R	Yes E	No	Yes U	Yes E	Yes CC
Michigan	Yes E	Yes E	Yes E	No	Yes E	Yes C
Minnesota	No	Yes	No	Yes	No	No
Mississippi D, E	No	Yes	No	Yes	Yes	No
Missouri	Yes D, E	Yes D, E	No	Yes D, E	Yes D, E	Yes D, E, X
Montana V	Y	Yes I	No	Yes M	Yes L	No
Nebraska	No	Yes	No	Yes	Yes	No
Nevada	No	Yes	No	Yes	Yes	No
New Hampshire	No	Yes E	No	No	Yes E	No
New Jersey	No	Yes E	No	Yes	Yes D, E	No
New Mexico	No	Yes	No	Yes E	Yes	No
New York	No	Yes E	No	No	No	No
North Carolina	Yes AA	Yes	No	Yes AA	Yes E	Yes AA
North Dakota	Yes	Yes	Yes E	Yes	Yes E	Yes
Ohio	No	Yes E	No	No	Yes D	No
Oklahoma	No H	Yes	No	Yes M	Yes L	No
Oregon	No	Yes	No	Yes M	Yes	No
Pennsylvania D, E	No	Yes	No	No	Yes F	No
Puerto Rico	O	O	—	O	O	—
Rhode Island	G, R	Yes	No	Yes	Yes E	No
South Carolina	Yes Z	Yes D	Yes T	Yes Z	Yes D	Yes T
South Dakota	No	No J	No	No	Yes E	No

Pharmacy Technicians in Community Setting (Continued)

State	May Pharmacy Technicians in the Community Setting:					
	Accept Called-In Rx from Physician's Office?	Enter Prescription into Computer?	Check the Work of Other Technicians?	Call Physician for Refill Authorization?	Compound Medications for Dispensing?	Transfer Prescriptions via Telephone?
Tennessee	Yes E, R	Yes E	No K	Yes	Yes E	Yes R
Texas	No	Yes	No	Yes M	Yes D, N	No
Utah	No	Yes E	No	Yes M	Yes E	Yes E
Vermont	No	Yes	No	Yes	Yes A, B	No
Virginia	No	Yes E	No	Yes M	Yes D, E	No
Washington	No	Yes	No	Yes M	Yes P	No
West Virginia	No	Yes D, E	No	Yes D, E	No	No
Wisconsin	Y, M	Yes	No	Yes M, Y	Yes B	No
Wyoming	D, E	No	Yes	N/A	Yes M	Yes E	No

Legend

A — Activities are not addressed in laws or statutes.

B — Subject to approved policy and procedure manuals, supportive personnel training, and pharmacist final verification and initialing.

C — Yes, if there are policies and procedures in place that allow delegation and that comply with Board Administrative Rules 338.490 and 338.3162.

D — Allowed activity must be under the direct supervision of a licensed pharmacist. (HI, "Immediate supervision." KY, Direct supervision if technician is not certified; if certified by the Pharmacy Technician Certification Board, then technician may perform activity under indirect supervision. LA, "Direct and immediate.")

E — Pharmacist must verify, check, and/or is responsible for allowed activities.

F — Compounding is the responsibility of the pharmacist or pharmacy intern under the direct supervision of the pharmacist. The pharmacist may utilize the assistance of supportive personnel under certain conditions. Contact board for requirements.

G — Unless it is regarding a refill.

H — Allowed activity limited to pharmacists and interns. (KY, Under direct supervision.)

I — Allowed activity must be under the supervision of a licensed pharmacist.

J — May key-in but not enter.

K — Possible revisions.

L — Bulk compounding allowed.

M — If there are any changes to the prescription and/or if professional consultation is involved, then the pharmacist must handle the call.

N — Must have special training. Contact the board for training requirements.

O — Pharmacy Act allows pharmacy assistants to perform the tasks assigned by the pharmacist under his/her supervision. PR Supreme Court has recognized that only pharmacists are prepared to do patient counseling.

P — Bulk compounding and intravenous preparation are allowed, but "extemporaneous" compounding is not allowed.

Q — Not prohibited. Law and regulations are silent on this issue; however, the practice is discouraged. Pharmacists should exercise professional judgment.

R — If technician is certified.

S — Pharmacist must verify, check, and/or is responsible for allowed activities; except in the case of Schedule II controlled substances, only a pharmacist may receive an oral prescription.

T — A supervising pharmacist may authorize a certified pharmacy technician to (1) receive and initiate verbal telephone orders; (2) conduct one-time prescription transfers; (3) check a technician's refill of medications if the medication is to be administered by a licensed health care professional in an institutional setting; (4) check a technician's repackaging of medication from bulk to unit dose in an institutional setting.

U — Provided no change in therapy.

V — Technicians can now work up to 30 minutes alone in the pharmacy while a pharmacist has a mandatory lunch break (up to 30 minutes) on the premises.

Pharmacy Technicians in Community Setting (Continued)

W — Pharmacy technician may call for refills for prescriptions other than controlled dangerous substances. May not accept refill authorization that changes the order.

X — May not transfer controlled substance prescriptions.

Y — Refills only with no changes. (WI, new prescriptions must be recorded.)

Z — Certified technicians only with supervising pharmacist authorization.

AA — Board-certified technicians only.

BB — May accept called-in prescription from physician office only if an advanced technician.

NABPLAW Online Search Terms (*type as indicated below*)
Pharmacy Technicians in Community Setting

- technician & requirements
- support & personnel & requirements
- technician & training
- technician & registration

Note: "ancillary personnel," "support personnel," and "nonlicensed personnel" can be substituted for "technician."

Appendix Seven

LEGAL STATUS OF FAX
PRESCRIPTIONS

Facsimile Transmission of Prescriptions

State	Has State Adopted Prescription Fax Regulations?	Controlled Substances Allowed	Internal Security Code Required	Transmission Marked: "Faxed Copy"
Alabama	Yes	Yes	No	No
Alaska	Yes	Yes	No	No
Arizona	No A	Yes	No	No
Arkansas	Yes	Yes, Sch. III–V F	No	No
California	Yes	Yes, Sch. III–V G	No	No
Colorado	Yes	Yes Z	No	No
Connecticut	Yes	Yes, Sch. II–V F	No	Yes
Delaware	Yes	Yes	No	Yes
District of Columbia	Pending	—	—	—
Florida	Yes	Yes, Sch. III–V & limited C-II	No	No
Georgia	Yes	Yes F	No	No
Guam	Yes E, I, J	Yes F	No	No
Hawaii	Yes K	Yes, Limited L	Yes M, L, K	No
Idaho	Yes	Yes F	No	No
Illinois	Yes A, N, P	Yes A, N, P	No	No
Indiana	Yes	Sch. III–V O, P	No	Yes
Iowa	Yes	Yes T	No	No
Kansas	Yes	Yes P	No	No
Kentucky	No A, Q	Yes P	A	A
Louisiana	Yes	Yes	No	No
Maine	Yes	Yes	No	No

State				
Maryland	Yes	Yes GG	No	No
Massachusetts	Yes FF	Yes JJ	No	Yes JJ
Michigan	Yes	Yes	No	No
Minnesota	Yes	Yes	No	No
Mississippi	Yes	Yes	No	No
Missouri	Yes	Yes S, T	Yes	Yes
Montana	Yes	Yes T	Yes X	Yes FF
Nebraska	Yes	Yes	No	No
Nevada	Yes F	Yes, Sch. III–V	No	Yes
New Hampshire	Yes	Yes	No	Yes BB
New Jersey	Yes	Yes, Sch. II–V B, EE	No	No
New Mexico	Yes	Yes	No	No
New York	Yes	No	No W	No
North Carolina	Yes	Yes	N/A	N/A
North Dakota	Yes	Yes, Sch. III–V	No	Yes
Ohio	Yes	Yes P	Yes	No
Oklahoma	Board guidelines A	Sch. II–V EE	No	No
Oregon	Board policy	Yes F	No	No
Pennsylvania	Yes	II	N/A	N/A
Puerto Rico	No	No	No	No
Rhode Island	Yes	Yes P	No	No
South Carolina	Yes Z	Yes U	No	—
South Dakota	Yes F	Yes F	No	Yes
Tennessee	Yes	Yes F	No	Yes
Texas	Yes A, Q	Yes P	No	Yes
Utah	Yes AA	No	No	Yes

Facsimile Transmission of Prescriptions (Continued)

State	Has State Adopted Prescription Fax Regulations?	Controlled Substances Allowed	Internal Security Code Required	Transmission Marked: "Faxed Copy"
Vermont	Yes	Yes, Sch. III–V	No	No
Virginia	Yes	Yes	No	Yes
Washington	Yes	Yes	No	No
West Virginia	Yes DD	Yes F	No	Yes KK
Wisconsin	Yes	Yes F	No	No
Wyoming	Yes	Yes P	R	Yes

Facsimile Transmission of Prescriptions (Continued)

State	Must Prescriber Information Appear?	Signature of Prescriber's Transmitting Agent	Nonfading Record-Legibility Time Requirement	Disposition of Original Prescription
Alabama	Yes	No	Yes	A, P
Alaska	Yes	Yes	Yes, 2 years	B
Arizona	Yes	No	Yes D	Not specified
Arkansas	Yes E	No	Yes	Not specified F
California	Yes	No	Yes, 3 years	Not specified
Colorado	Yes	No	Yes, 2 years	Not specified
Connecticut	Yes E	No	Yes	H
Delaware	Yes	No	No	F (for C-II)
District of Columbia	—	—	—	—
Florida	Yes	No	No	J
Georgia	Yes	Yes	No	Not addressed
Guam	Yes	No	Not addressed HH	Not addressed HH
Hawaii	Yes	No, prescriber only	Yes, 5 years	Not specified
Idaho	Yes	No	Yes	F
Illinois	No A	No A	Yes	A, N
Indiana	Yes	Yes, name	Yes	Not specified T
Iowa	Yes	No LL	Yes, 2 years	Not specified T
Kansas	Yes	No	Yes, 5 years	Not specified
Kentucky	A	A	A	A
Louisiana	Yes	No	Yes D, 2 years	Not specified
Maine	Yes	No W	Yes, 5 years	Board policy

Facsimile Transmission of Prescriptions (Continued)

State	Must Prescriber Information Appear?	Signature of Prescriber's Transmitting Agent	Nonfading Record–Legibility Time Requirement	Disposition of Original Prescription
Maryland	Yes R	No	Yes, 5 years	GG
Massachusetts	Yes	No	No longer referenced	Not specified JJ
Michigan	Yes	No	Yes, 5 years	J
Minnesota	Yes	Yes	Yes, 5 years	B
Mississippi	Yes	No	Yes	B, I
Missouri	Yes	Yes	No	Retained by practitioner T
Montana	Yes	Yes	Yes, 2 years	Retained by practitioner
Nebraska	F	No	F	F
Nevada	Yes E	No E	Yes, 2 years	Not specified
New Hampshire	Yes	No	No	I, F
New Jersey	Yes	No	Yes	Not specified
New Mexico	Yes	Name required V	Yes, 3 years	Not specified F
New York	Yes	No	Yes, 5 years	Not specified
North Carolina	Yes	Yes	Yes	N/A
North Dakota	Yes	No	Yes, 5 years	I, T
Ohio	Yes	Yes, ID required	Yes Y	Retained by prescriber
Oklahoma	Yes	No	No	N/A
Oregon	Yes	Name or initials F	Yes, 3 years	No
Pennsylvania	Yes	No	Yes, 3 years	II
Puerto Rico	N/A	N/A	N/A	N/A
Rhode Island	Yes	No	No	Not specified

State				
South Carolina	Yes	No	Not addressed	Not specified
South Dakota	Yes	No	Yes	F
Tennessee	Yes	No	Yes	Not specified
Texas	Yes	Name required	Yes	Not specified
Utah AA	Yes	No	Yes	Not specified GG
Vermont	Yes	—	—	—
Virginia	Yes	No C	Yes CC	Retained by practitioner
Washington	Yes	No	Yes, 2 years	Not specified
West Virginia	Yes	No E, W	No	Not specified F, D
Wisconsin	Same as written Rx	No	Yes	Not specified
Wyoming	Yes R	Yes, or initials	Yes	Patient files

Legend

A — A faxed prescription is handled in the same manner as a phoned-in prescription. (IL, Faxing of C-IIs is under the same restriction as telephone orders in emergency situations. KY, "Oral" prescription.)

B — Original, signed prescription must be presented before the faxed, filled prescription is released to the patient. (AK, IA, MD, MN, MS, NH, C-II prescriptions.)

C — Yes, if fax is used to transmit an oral prescription and prescription is not manually signed by the prescriber.

D — Must be reduced to hardcopy if necessary that indicates mode of transmission and prescriber's phone number.

E — Prescriber's signature must appear.

F — Faxed prescriptions are permitted as per Drug Enforcement Administration (DEA) regulation. 21 Code of Federal Regulations §1306.11 and 1306.21.

G — In handwriting of the prescriber for C-III to C-V.

H — Retained or destroyed by a practitioner.

I — Fax becomes original (not C-II).

J — If fax is prescriber generated, then fax is original. If fax is other generated (patient), then original to pharmacy before delivering to patient.

Facsimile Transmission of Prescriptions (Continued)

K — Jurisdiction: Department of Health, Food and Drug Branch.

L — Jurisdiction: Department of Public Safety, Narcotics Enforcement Division.

M — Practitioner oral code number.

N — Faxing allowed for all but C-II. Photocopying or immediately reducing prescription to writing is required to produce a non-fading record.

O — Schedule III–V may only be sent from an institutional facility by the authorizing practitioner or an authorized agent.

P — Schedule II permitted only for home infusion prescriptions, long-term care facility (LTCF) inpatients, and hospice patients. (AL and KS, All other C-II prescriptions may be faxed, but original must be presented to pharmacist before medication can be dispensed. TX, The Schedule II prescription faxed must be a properly completed official prescription form.)

Q — However, the State Controlled Substance Act allows the faxing of C-II controlled substance prescriptions in certain circumstances.

R — Signature of prescriber; location from which the prescription was faxed, including address, phone number, and fax number; and pharmacy information must also include telephone number and fax number.

S — Bureau of Narcotics and Dangerous Drugs.

T — C-II requires original prescription at time of prescription pickup except for prescriptions for long-term care and hospice patients and those written for parenteral narcotic drugs and emergency dispensing.

U — Hospice, long-term care, and home infusion patients only. For C-II prescriptions only.

V — For verbal confirmation.

W — Pharmacists are responsible for assessing authenticity.

X — Electronic signature or other secure (encrypted or encoded) method of validation; both prescriber and pharmacist must have a secure (encrypted or encoded) system.

Y — Three years from date of last refill; maximum of four years.

Z — Pharmacist may accept an electronically transmitted order.

AA — Prescription must be transmitted by fax from site of origination to the dispensing pharmacy.

BB — By the receiving pharmacist (and initialed).

CC — Two years from date of last refill; maximum of four years.

DD — Under regulations regarding electronic transmission of prescriptions.

EE — A prescription for a Schedule II drug written for a LTCF resident or hospice patient does not have to be in writing and signed by the practitioner if it is transmitted or prepared in compliance with the DEA regulations 21 CFR §1306.11 (d), (e), (f), and (g).

FF — Regulations for all electronically issued prescriptions.

GG — Fax prescriptions accepted as originals unless Food and Drug Administration or DEA restrictions apply, as in Schedule II in some instances.

HH — State is in the process of promulgating new regulations.

II — Board Regulation section 27.20 should be reviewed for the specific requirements and limitations.

JJ — Faxed prescriptions are permitted as per DEA regulation.

KK — But only for controlled substances.

LL — Name required.

**NABPLAW Online Search Terms *(type as indicated below)*
Facsimile Transmission of Prescriptions**

- facsimile & transmission
- prescription & transmission
- prescription & records & facsimile

Appendix Eight

WHO HAS PRESCRIBING AUTHORITY

Prescribing Authority

State	Doctor of Homeopathy (Limited to Course of Practice)	Physician Assistant	Advanced Registered Nurse Practitioner	Clinical Nurse Specialist	Nurse Midwife
Alabama	D	H	H	E	H
Alaska	E	B	A*	E*	E*
Arizona	A*	B, H	A	*	E*
Arkansas	E	B	A*	A*	A*
California*	E	B	B	E	B
Colorado	A*	B	A*	B	H
Connecticut	E	B, H	A*	E	A*
Delaware	D	B	A*	A*	A*
District of Columbia	D	B	A*	A*	A*
Florida	D	B*	B*	E	E
Georgia	D	B	B	E	B
Guam	A	H	E	H*	H*
Hawaii	D, E	H*	H	H	H
Idaho	D	B*	*	*	*
Illinois	E	B	B	B	B
Indiana	D	E	B*	B*	B*
Iowa	D	H*	A	E*	E*
Kansas	E	B	B	E	E
Kentucky	D	H*	H*	H*	H*
Louisiana	D	H	H	H	H

State					
Maine	E	B	A	E	A
Maryland	E	B	B*	E	B*
Massachusetts	E*	B	B*	B*	B*
Michigan	D	B	B	B	B
Minnesota	D, E	B	B	B	A
Mississippi	D	B	B	C	B
Missouri	E	B*	B*	B*	B*
Montana	E	B	A*	A*	A*
Nebraska*	D	B	A*	A*	B*
Nevada	A	B	B	E	E
New Hampshire	E	A	A	E	E
New Jersey	D	B, H	B, H	E	B, H
New Mexico	E	B	A, H*	A, H*	A, H*
New York	D, E	B	A	E	E (see midwife)
North Carolina*	E	B	E	E	B
North Dakota*	D	B	A	A	A
Ohio	D	E	D*	D*	D*
Oklahoma	E	B, H	B, H	B, H	B, H (certified)
Oregon	D	B	A*	E	A*
Pennsylvania	D, E	H*	H*	E	E
Puerto Rico	E	E	H	E	E
Rhode Island	E	B	B	B, H	B*
South Carolina	E	B*	B*	B*	B*
South Dakota*	E	B	B	E	B
Tennessee	E	A	A	A	A
Texas	D	B*	B*	B*	B*

Prescribing Authority (Continued)

State	Doctor of Homeopathy (Limited to Course of Practice)	Physician Assistant	Advanced Registered Nurse Practitioner	Clinical Nurse Specialist	Nurse Midwife
Utah	D	B	A*	E	A*
Vermont	D	B	A*	B*	B*
Virginia	E	B, H*	B, H	E	B, H
Washington	D	B	A*	—	A
West Virginia	E	B, H	H	E	H
Wisconsin	E	B	A	E	E
Wyoming	D	B	A*	E*	E*

* See Footnotes (*) on pages 179–185 .

Prescribing Authority (Continued)

State	Nurse Practitioner	OB/GYN Nurse Practitioner	Pediatric Nurse Practitioner	Psychiatric Nurse Practitioner	Certified Registered Nurse Anesthetist
Alabama	H	H	H	H	E
Alaska	A*	A*	A*	A*	A*
Arizona	A	A	A	A	E*
Arkansas	E*	*	*	A*	E*
California	B	B	B	B	E
Colorado	B	B	B	B	B
Connecticut	A*	A*	A*	A*	A*
Delaware	A*	A*	A*	A*	A*
District of Columbia	A*	A*	A*	A*	E
Florida	E	E	E	E	E
Georgia	B	B	B	B	E
Guam	H*	H*	H*	H*	H*
Hawaii	H	H	H	H	H
Idaho	*	*	*	*	*
Illinois	B	D, E	D, E	D, E	B
Indiana	B*	B*	B*	B*	B
Iowa	E*	E*	E*	E*	A*
Kansas	E*	E	E	E	E
Kentucky	H*	H*	H*	H*	H*
Louisiana	H	H	H	H	H
Maine	A	A	A	A	E

Prescribing Authority (Continued)

State	Nurse Practitioner	OB/GYN Nurse Practitioner	Pediatric Nurse Practitioner	Psychiatric Nurse Practitioner	Certified Registered Nurse Anesthetist
Maryland	B*	B*	B*	B*	E
Massachusetts	B	B	B	B	E
Michigan	B	B	B	B	B
Minnesota	B	B	B	B	B
Mississippi	B	B	B	B	B
Missouri	B*	B*	B*	B*	B*
Montana	A*	A*	A*	A*	E
Nebraska	A*	A*	A*	A*	A*
Nevada	E	E	E	E	E
New Hampshire	A	A	A	A	A
New Jersey	B, H	E	E	E	E
New Mexico	A, H*	A, H*	A, H*	A, H*	A, H*
New York	A*	A	A	A	E
North Carolina	B	B	B	B	E
North Dakota	A	A	A	A	A
Ohio	D*	D*	D*	D*	C
Oklahoma	E	E	E	E	B, H
Oregon	A*	A*	A*	A*	C
Pennsylvania	H*	H*	H*	H*	E
Puerto Rico*	E	E	E	E	E
Rhode Island	B*	E	E	E	E

South Carolina	B*	B*	B*	B*	E
South Dakota	B	B	B	B	E
Tennessee	A	A	A	A	E
Texas	B*	B*	B*	B*	B*
Utah	A*	A*	A*	A*	E
Vermont	B	B	B	B	B
Virginia	B, H*	B, H	B, H	B, H	E
Washington	A	A	A	A	A
West Virginia	E	E	E	E	E
Wisconsin	E	E	E	E	E
Wyoming	E*	E*	E*	E*	E*

* See Footnotes (*) on pages 179–185.

Prescribing Authority (Continued)

State	Midwife	Optometrist	Emergency Medical Technician Paramedic	Naturopathic Doctor
Alabama	E	H	E	D
Alaska	C, E	F, H	C	E
Arizona	E*	A, Limited	E	H
Arkansas	E	A, Limited	E	E
California	E	H	C	B
Colorado	E	H*	E	E*
Connecticut	E	A	E	E
Delaware	E	A, G, H*	E	D
District of Columbia	B	A	C	E
Florida	E	A, Limited formulary	E	A*
Georgia	E	A, Limited formulary*	E	E
Guam	H*	H*	E	E
Hawaii	H	H	E	H*
Idaho	E	A	C	A*
Illinois	D	F, G, H	E	E
Indiana	B	H, Limited formulary*	E	E
Iowa	E	A*	E	D
Kansas	E	H*	C	B
Kentucky	E	H*	C	E
Louisiana	H	H	E	D
Maine	A	H	C	H

Maryland	E	H*	E	E
Massachusetts	E*	H*	E	E
Michigan	E	H	E	D
Minnesota	E	H	C	D, E
Mississippi	C	H*	C	E
Missouri	E	H	E	E
Montana	E	H	E	H
Nebraska	B*	A, Limited*	E	D
Nevada	E	H	C	E
New Hampshire	C	A, H	E	H
New Jersey	B, H	H	E	D
New Mexico	E	A, H	C	E
New York	A*	A	E	E
North Carolina	B	A	E	E
North Dakota	A, Limited	H	E	D
Ohio	E	A, Limited	E	D
Oklahoma	E	A	E	E
Oregon	E	A, Limited	C	A*
Pennsylvania	E	F, G, H*	E	D, E
Puerto Rico	E	E	E	—
Rhode Island	E	H	C	D
South Carolina	E	A, Limited*	E	E
South Dakota	E	A, Limited	E	E
Tennessee	E	A	E	E
Texas	C	A, Limited formulary	C	D
Utah	H	H	D, E	A*

Prescribing Authority (Continued)

State	Midwife	Optometrist	Emergency Medical Technician Paramedic	Naturopathic Doctor
Vermont	B*	A, G	C	H*
Virginia	E	A, H	E	E
Washington	C	F, G	C	H*
West Virginia	E	H	C	E
Wisconsin	E	H	E	E
Wyoming	E	H	C	D

* See Footnotes (*) on pages 179–185.

Medical doctors have unlimited, independent prescribing authority in every state.

Doctors of osteopathy have unlimited, independent prescribing authority in all states except Puerto Rico, where they have no prescribing authority.

Doctors of dental surgery, doctors of pediatric medicine, and doctors of veterinary medicine have independent prescribing authority that is limited to their course of practice in every state.

Doctors of chiropractic have no prescribing authority in any state.

Legend

A — Independent authority

B — Dependent prescribing authority

C — Use only

D — Not licensed

E — No prescribing authority
F — Diagnostic only
G — Therapeutics
H — Limited prescribing authority

Footnotes (*)

AK — Advanced nurse practitioners (ANP) may prescribe and dispense within the scope of their specialty.

AR — "Advanced practice registered nurses" (APRNs) must be certified under rules promulgated by the Arkansas State Board of Nursing. All APRNs have independent prescribing authority if they are licensed as APRNs, have obtained a Drug Enforcement Administration (DEA) number, and maintain a collaborative agreement with a physician licensed in AR whose background and active practice corresponds with that of the advanced practice nurse. The area of prescriptive authority is limited to that of education and certification. The ANP, certified nurse midwife (CNM), clinical nurse specialist (CNS), and certified registered nurse anesthetist (CRNA) all fall under the category of APRN. There is a category of nurse practitioners (NPs) that is not considered an APRN and therefore does not have prescriptive authority. Currently, AR does not have any CRNAs who have opted for prescriptive authority but would function independently. Midwives are licensed by the state health department and have no prescriptive authority.

AZ — Homeopathic physician has prescriber authority. Title of "clinical nurse specialist" not used. Nurse midwife is used if also NP.

CA — Dependent prescribing authority for CNM and certified NP. Dependent prescribing authority for pharmacists in licensed health facilities, clinics, health maintenance organizations (HMOs), and providers contracting with HMOs in accordance with policies, procedures, or protocols.

Prescribing Authority (Continued)

CO — Homeopathic physicians have prescriptive authority if they are a medical doctor or doctor of osteopathy. A naturopathic doctor would have no such authority, except for vitamins, minerals, and the like. Advanced practice nurses have independent authority if they are approved by the nursing board, have obtained a DEA number, and maintain a collaborative agreement with a physician licensed in CO whose background and active practice corresponds with that of the nurse. Optometrists may purchase, possess, administer, and prescribe certain pharmaceutical agents for examination and treatment if they are therapeutically certified by the Optometric Examiners Board.

CT — Advanced practice nurses have independent authority if they are licensed as APRNs, have obtained a DEA number, and maintain a collaborative agreement with a physician licensed in CT whose background and active practice corresponds with that of the advanced practice nurse. The NP, pediatric nurse practitioner, psychiatric nurse practitioner, and certified nurse anesthetist all fall under the category of advanced registered nurse practitioner (ARNP).

DC — Only NPs, CNSs, nurse midwives, and nurse anesthetists who are licensed by the DC Board of Nursing as an APRN have independent prescribing authority.

DE — Advanced practice nurses must be licensed by the Board of Nursing and must submit a collaborative care agreement to the Joint Practice Committee. Optometrists must be therapeutically certified to prescribe.

FL — For physician assistants (PAs), there exists a limited formulary. APRNs may initiate orders under protocol. Naturopathic doctors have unlimited prescribing authority.

GA — Optometrists may prescribe from a specific formulary.

GU — Optometrists may prescribe from a limited formulary. APRNs must have a collaborative practice agreement with MD.

HI — Naturopathic doctors may prescribe vitamins, minerals, amino acids, and fatty acids. PAs have full prescription authority under the supervision of a licensed physician, with the exception of Schedule II controlled substances. PAs may only prescribe Schedule II controlled substances in hospitals or extended care facilities. Nurses can prescribe controlled substances with supervision. Pharmacists may adjust dosage regimens pursuant to prescriber authorization. Prescription of therapeutic pharmaceuticals as approved by the Board of Examiners in Optometry is allowed.

IA — "Certified" CNS, "certified" nurse midwives, and "certified" NP (ARNP classifications) have independent prescribing authority. PAs must have supervising physician and prescriptive authority; does not include C-II stimulants or depressants. Two classes of optometrists: (1) certified licensed optometrists can use some drugs for diagnostic purposes only; (2) therapeutically certified optometrists can prescribe but not dispense (except at no charge to commence a course of therapy) drugs relating to the treatment of ocular diseases or conditions.

ID — PAs, NPs, CNMs, CNSs, and registered nurse anesthetists all have independent prescribing authority limited to scope of practice and must be approved to prescribe by their respective boards. PAs have supervising physician. Naturopathic doctors have independent authority only if approved by formulary council.

IN — Advanced practice nurses" must be certified under rules promulgated by the Board of Nursing and Medical Licensing Board. When certified, they will have dependent authority. Must have collaborative agreement with physician and may only prescribe within the scope of the physician's practice. The state does not necessarily recognize each listed nursing specialty. Hospital and private mental institutional pharmacists may adjust drug therapies pursuant to protocol and under the supervision of a physician. Optometrists must be certified by a committee of the Pharmacy Board and use formularies to prescribe. They may not prescribe for controlled substances.

KS — Not unless they are an ARNP, but these designations alone do not have any authority. Optometrist licensed as therapeutic licensee or diagnostic and therapeutic licensee. Naturopathic doctor may prescribe pursuant to a protocol with a physician."

Prescribing Authority (Continued)

KY — Pharmacists may initiate, continue, or discontinue drug therapy pursuant to an established collaborative care agreement. Pharmacists who enter into a collaborative care agreement with a practitioner may cooperatively manage a patient's drug-related health care needs. The agreement shall be limited to specification of the drug-related regimen and necessary tests; stipulated conditions for initiating, continuing, or discontinuing drug therapy; and directions concerning the monitoring of drug therapy and conditions warranting dose, dosage regimen, dosage form, or route of administration modifications. ARNPs who prescribe must enter into a written collaborative practice agreement with a physician that defines scope of prescriptive authority. ARNPs cannot prescribe controlled substances. Optometrists may prescribe diagnostic topical medications for use in the eye or its appendages. "Therapeutically certified" optometrists may prescribe oral medications, except C-I and C-II controlled substances, for any condition that an optometrist is authorized to treat under KRS 320. The authority to prescribe C-III, C-IV, and C-V controlled substances shall be limited to prescriptions for a quantity sufficient to provide treatment for up to 72 hours. No refills of prescriptions for controlled substances are allowed. PAs cannot prescribe controlled substances.

MA — MA only recognizes registered nurse practitioners. CNS prescribing authority is for psychiatric nurse specialists only. Nurse midwife prescribing authority is for CNM only. Optometrists may prescribe topical Schedule VI drugs for use in the eye but may not prescribe glaucoma medications.

MD — Certified registered nurse practitioners (including specialties) and nurse midwives may only prescribe within their specialty. Nurse midwives have a limited formulary. A therapeutically certified optometrist may prescribe under certain conditions.

MO — Must have a collaborative practice arrangement with a physician.

MS — Optometrists may prescribe topicals and drugs only for treatment and diseases of the eye and its adnexa.

MT — NP, pediatric nurse practitioner, psychiatric nurse practitioner, and certified nurse anesthetist all fall under the category of ARNP. Pharmacist's prescribing authority based on a collaborative practice agreement with a physician.

NC — Clinical pharmacist practitioners have dependent prescribing authority.

ND — Pharmacist's prescribing authority based on a collaborative practice agreement with a physician.

NE — Some apply for prescribing authority, not automatic. Optometrists may prescribe topical ocular pharmaceutical agents and oral medications that are within their scope of practice.

NM — The Board of Nursing determines by certification which specialties have prescriptive authority. CNMs prescribe pursuant to Department of Health rules. For pharmacist clinicians only, in accordance with the NM Pharmacist Prescriptive Authority Act.

NY — Nurse practitioners" are authorized to issue prescriptions in accordance with practice agreements and practice protocols between the physician and NP. Effective 1994, implementation of the Midwifery Practice Act resulted in licensure of professional midwives.

OH — Only advanced practice nurses licensed by the Nursing Board may prescribe drugs under certain conditions and within a limited formulary.

OR — NPs may prescribe independently, but only for drugs allowed by formulary for their area of practice. Naturopaths may only prescribe, administer, and dispense nonpoisonous plant and animal substances as determined by a formulary council in therapeutic dosages; they may administer select anesthetics, antiseptics, and radiopaque substances.

PA — As and NPs based on formulary and written agreement with supervising physician. Please contact the Osteopathic Medical Board, Medical Board, and/or Nursing Board for specific requirements and current status of laws/regulations. Optometrists, additional requirements for a Board of Optometry therapeutic license.

RI — Nurse midwives must be CNMs to prescribe, and NPs must be certified nurse practitioners to prescribe. Optometrists limited to topical ophthalmics.

Prescribing Authority (Continued)

SC — As are certified by Board of Medical Examiners for prescriptive authority and formulary. Extended role of NP certified by Nursing Board; under approved protocol from Nursing Board. Optometrists are therapeutically certified by the Board of Examiners in Optometry for limited prescriptive authority.

SD — A statute passed in 1993 allows pharmacists to initiate or modify drug therapy by protocol or other legal authority established and approved within a licensed health care facility or by a practitioner authorized to prescribe drugs.

TX — PAs and registered nurses (RNs) who have advanced training may prescribe per protocol with a practitioner dangerous drugs and 30-day supply of controlled substance III–V with no refills. PAs must be recognized by the Medical Board and have specialized training and education. RNs must be recognized by the Nursing Board and have specialized training and education. Pharmacists may perform specific acts relating to drug therapy management under written protocol from a practitioner including implementing or modifying therapy.

UT — APRNs can prescribe C-IIs and C-IIIs with consultation. Naturopathic doctors must prescribe pursuant to a specific formulary.

VA — In VA, NPs and PAs who have applied, met criteria, and been approved for prescriptive authority may prescribe and possess Schedule III–V and legend drugs that have been approved by the supervising medical practitioner.

VT — Contact the Board of Nursing for specific prescribing requirements. Naturopaths may prescribe pursuant to their formulary.

WA — Clinical nurse specialist" is not a recognized designation in this state. All other NPs are included in ARNP classification. ARNPs have independent authority for legend drugs and controlled substances. Naturopathic practitioners may prescribe a limited number of legend drugs, including vitamins, minerals, whole gland thyroid, vitamin B$_{12}$ preparations, antibiotics, corticosteroids, and the like. (List available from Washington State Board of Pharmacy.) Legislation enacted in 2005 allows the prescribing of limited controlled substances when an approved drug list is developed. Optometrists may prescribe for conditions of the eye subject to certain training requirements. Limited oral drugs were authorized and injectable epinephrine in 2004, including some controlled substances.

WY — Prescribing authority only for those designated as APRN. May be certified in specialty areas indicated with an asterisk (*). APRN may prescribe controlled substances (C-II to C-V).

INDEX